ST. MICHAEL'S COLLEGE SERIES

— 1 —

COVER:
SIMONE CANTARINI (IL PESARESE), *SIBILLA*. PESARO, BANCA POPOLARE DELL'ADRIATICO

St. Michael's College. From Architect's Drawing, 1852

Going for Baroque

Cultural Transformations 1550-1650

Proceedings of
A St. Michael's College Symposium
(27-28 February 1998)

Edited by

Francesco Guardiani

LEGAS

New York Ottawa Toronto

Canadian Cataloguing in Publication Data

Main entry under title:

Going for Baroque: cultural transformations ca. 1550-1650

Papers presented at a St. Michael's College Symposium, Feb. 27-28, 1998
Includes bibliographical references

ISBN 0-921252-88-9

1. Europe-- Intellectual Life -- Congresses. 2. Civilization, Baroque -- Congresses. I. Guardiani Francesco, 1949-

CB401.G64 1999 940.2'2 C98-901456-8

For further information and for orders:

LEGAS

P. O. Box 040328	68 Kamloops Ave.	2908 Dufferin Street
Brooklyn, New York	Ottawa, Ontario	Toronto, Ontario
USA 11204	K1V 7C9	M6B 3S8

Printed and bound in Canada

A St. Michael's College Symposium

St. Michael's College is a Catholic Liberal Arts College within the University of Toronto. This means that it bears a double portion of groans and travails: those which afflict Liberal Arts Colleges everywhere in this uncertain age, and the ones particular to Catholic academic institutions, which so often seem to fall between too many stools to enjoy any comfort at all. Although it traces its birth "to the heart of the Church," and despite its memories of participation in "a course of tradition which may be traced back to the very origin of the university as an institution," the College is far from certain about what all this may entail for its present and its future.

We all know that the large issues are going to take some time to clarify in any fruitful way. Those of us who live and work in an institution like St. Michael's now could wait until things become clear again. Or we can pursue humble aims which have not yet been made entirely unattainable by our anxieties and uncertainties. The cultivation of a modicum of conviviality, both intellectual and of the other kind, is still possible even in our reduced circumstances. And so the idea was born to begin, at the College, the experiment of a yearly Symposium around a theme which seems likely to engage the attention of a number of the College's Fellows.

It must be said that the first such Symposium, whose Proceedings, o Reader, you are now fortunate to have in your hands, was a joy. It proved that, whatever the vicissitudes to which we have been subject in recent years, it is indeed still possible to share in what the Pope calls "that *gaudium de veritate*, so precious to St. Augustine, which is that joy of searching for, discovering and communicating truth in every field of knowledge." Unlikely as the Baroque may have at first appeared as a theme capable of eliciting such joy, it did; and this is evident, we believe, in the papers before you. We believe, too, that the inter-disciplinarity of the College's members has produced a variety of perspectives which is fruitful and unusual in volumes of this sort.

We hope that the experiment will continue, and that each future Symposium will prove even more joyful than the first. A second one, on Medievalism, has already been planned and a third one on hagiography has been proposed. May the series of volumes like this one grow long and serve as a *medium* and a sign of St. Michael's College academic conviviality.

Meanwhile, let us close by remembering gratefully the unfailing support which Professor Mariel O'Neill-Karsh, Acting Principal of the College, as she then was, extended to this enterprise.

Joseph Goering
Francesco Guardiani
Giulio Silano

CONTENTS

Introduction:
An Idea of Baroque

SET BETWEEN THE END OF THE RENAISSANCE and the beginning of the Age of Reason, Baroque has traditionally appeared as a puzzling epoch to the student in arts and science, an age filled with unresolved ambiguities, divisive issues, and unsubstantiated projections of new values to replace established truths. **AND YET, IN THIS PERIOD,** we find some of the greatest achievements of modern culture in the Western world: the works of Galileo, Giovan Battista Marino, Giordano Bruno and Tommaso Campanella in Italy, Bacon and Shakespeare in England, Montaigne, D'Aubigné and Tristan l'Hermite in France, Gongora, Lope and Cervantes in Spain. What these authors have in common is that they are all agents of change, of an epochal transformation which also takes place in the arts with Caravaggio, Bernini, Borromini, or in the area of religion and historiography, with the Council of Trent and its two opposite "reports" to posterity, by Paolo Sarpi and Sforza Pallavicino. And, of course, "change" is the keyword in music to explain *la seconda pratica* of the "divine" Claudio Monteverdi or the unsurpassed innovations set by Girolamo Frescobaldi on the harpsichord. **THIS IS ALSO THE TIME OF NEW SPECIALIZAZIONS** in all of science as well as in the humanities, with the definition, the establishment and the printing of vocabularies, encyclopedias and manuals prescribing rules for the man of science or the newly coined "man of letters." And yet this is also the time of syncretism in the arts, with the birth of the musical-poetic-dramatic opera, and the multilayered tragedy of Adonis's myth in Ronsard, Shakespeare, and Marino. **THIS WORLD TURMOIL WAS DESCRIBED BY THE LATE MARSHALL MCLUHAN**, one of St. Michael's College's most distinguished professors, as an age of "blitz and metamorphoses," as the old aural world of manuscript culture met the new analytical, and mechanical world of print that was "rolling off the press". **TODAY WE FIND OURSELVES** in another period of intense cultural transformation. For well over a century we have used electric circuitry in our daily life (from telegraph to telephone, from radio to television), but it is only now, with the computer, that this technology has reached the level of a new cultural dimension enveloping us fully. **THE IMPULSE FOR CHANGE** from print to electricity, with all the cultural implications outlined in the *Gutenberg Galaxy* and *Understanding Media*, has never been more real than at the present time. There are sixty million subscribers to *Internet* worldwide and the figure is growing by the hundreds of thousands daily. We see glimpses of a new world in these effects, but we are still attached to the world we know better. This is the condition that reproduces the cultural interface of the Baroque era with its hybridism, multidisciplinarity and multimediality. The authors and artists we mentioned are placed between the ancient and the modern as we are between the modern and something else which, for lack of critical imagination, has been called "postmodern." **THE FIRST TRANSFORMATION** was marked by the passage from the aural world of manuscript culture to the visually biased world of perfect repeatability and mechanism created by print culture; the second is taking us away from mechanical modernity toward the new ethereal and, perhaps, more spiritual, dimension of cyberspace. They are different transformations (even though for some futurologists the new ideal world has already shown sign of a great return to the Middle Ages), but the mechanisms of the interface or, with a more appropriate metaphor, "the circuits" of the interface, remain quite the same. **THE AIM OF OUR WORK**, then, with the conference and with these proceedings, is to re-create a mosaic of cultural activities in the Baroque period, in order to detect the pattern of transformation that may well be the key to a better understanding of our yet to be defined present cultural condition. **F.G.**

Joseph Goering

Point of View: An Intellectual Revolution of the Baroque Age

ABSTRACT. Artists and artisans of the Baroque were fascinated with visual perspective and point-of-view. It was in this period that the tricks of perspective were mastered and its effects most thoroughly explored, and this mastery established an artistic culture that would shape western perceptions of reality until the twentieth century. This paper will suggest that, simultaneously with the artistic mastery of perspective and point of view, came an even more revolutionary notion that philosophical, theological and political opinion, like works of art, were expressions of an author's individual point of view. Thus were created "schools" of philosophy and theology (Aristotelianism, Thomism, Scotism, Augustinianism, Jansenism) and of politics (Gallicanism, Ultramontanism) each defined by its point of view on various key issues.

It is said of the Florentine painter, Paolo Uccello (1397-1475), "that the discovery of perspective had so impressed him that he spent nights and days drawing objects in foreshortening, and setting himself ever new problems. His fellow artists used to tell how he was so engrossed in these studies that he would hardly look up when his wife called him for a meal, and would just exclaim: 'What a sweet thing perspective is!'"(Gombrich 1951, 183).

The discovery of the laws of perspective and the effect created by painting from a fixed and particular point of view was perhaps the most original and momentous invention of the Renaissance. The ancient Greeks had understood foreshortening, and Hellenestic painters were skilled in creating the illusion of depth, but not before the fifteenth century were the tricks mastered of representing the external world in art according to scientific perspective and from fixed points of view (*ibid.* 164-65). The Florentine artist Filippo Brunelleschi (d. 1446) is often credited with being the first to apply the mathematical laws of perspective systematically, and other Florentines—Massaccio, Donatello, and, of course, Uccello—followed diligently in his

Going for Baroque: Cultural Transformations1550-1650.
A St. Michael's College Symposium. Francesco Guardiani ed. Ottawa: Legas, 1999

footsteps. Nor was this interest and delight in representing nature exactly as it appeared to an onlooker an Italian monopoly. Jan van Eyck (d. 1441), a contemporary of Brunelleschi, was exploring the same techniques, as were almost all of his contemporaries in the North. When he signed the picture known as "The Betrothal of the Arnolfini" with the words "I was here" (*Johannes de Eyck fuit hic*) he was vouching not so much for the legal validity of the human exchange depicted there, as for the historical and scientific accuracy, and thus the authority, of his eye-witness painted account (*ibid.* 173).

The success of this new way of representing reality as that which can be seen and measured and thus depicted with scientific precision took Europe by storm. By 1525 Albrecht Dürer could write a textbook (*Die Unterweissung der Messung*) on perspective and foreshortening, illustrating it with such famous woodcuts as "The painter Studying the Laws of Foreshortening by Means of Threads and a Frame" (*ibid.* 264). No successful artist from that time onward could afford to be ignorant of the techniques for producing the illusion of reality based on a fixed and personal point of view. This new way of seeing the world was internalized and came to seem "natural" and obvious to all.[1] Older ways of representing reality came gradually to be dismissed as primitive, immature and, of course, "medieval."

During the Baroque, these Renaissance tricks of scientific visual representation were mastered and their effects thoroughly explored. The techniques were tested and artists toyed with the visual effects made possible by manipulating them. But for all of their playfulness and exploration, none of the artists of the Baroque was willing or able to imagine depicting the natural world in an old-fashioned or medieval mode, one which ignored the laws of a fixed and individual perspective. Only with William Blake in the late eighteenth century (Gombrich 1951, 368), and then nearly a century later with Cezanne and the modernists (*ibid.* 405-411), would artists consciously turn their backs on these "laws" of representation, and become willing to

[1] See Gombrich, *Art and Illusion*, esp. Part Three: "The Beholder's Share" (153-244). On the importance of the viewer's collaboration with the artist to produce the illusion of reality in a painting, see ch. 8: "Ambiguities of the Third Dimension." Gombrich quotes with approval Sir Herbert Read, for example: "We do not always realize that the theory of perspective developed in the fifteenth century is a scientific convention; it is merely one way of describing space and has no absolute validity" (209).

sacrifice "linear perspective" and what had come to be known as "correct drawing" for other values.

The purpose of this brief communication is to explore the implications of this artistic revolution for the intellectual history of the Baroque period and for that of our own time. I wish to suggest that the internalization of these new principles of perspective and point-of-view had implications also for intellectual history. Just as it became usual to "read" works of art in terms of their point-of-view and perspective, so it came to be commonplace to assume that all philosophical, theological, and political opinions were, like visual artifacts, expressions of an author's individual point of view. Thus was born the possibility of "source criticism" (the scientific description of the various sources of a doctrine or a text, each having its own idiosyncratic perspective and thus its own discrete value), the "history of ideas" (including the notion that an individual author's point of view was constantly changing and was thus in need of careful description: the young and the old Augustine, or Luther, for example), and the historical-critical method of which the Renaissance philologists were the early harbingers. Thus too, were created "schools" of philosophy and theology (Aristotelianism, Thomism, Scotism, Augustinianism, Jansenism) and of politics (Gallicanism, Ultramontanism), each defined by its point of view on various key issues.

The results of this expansion of the realm of visual perspective and point of view into the teachings of the other arts and sciences were far-reaching, if largely unremarked at the time, or indeed for the next four centuries. The rejection of the medieval and ancient way of viewing the world of thought was as powerful as, and has proven even more tenacious than, the new ways of representing reality introduced by the Renaissance artists. We are the inheritors of these ways of thinking; they still seem to us self-evident, and thus it remains very difficult to imagine viable alternatives, either in the past, or in the present.[2]

Let me suggest with two examples some of the ways in which sixteenth and seventeenth century intellectual life was revolutionized by this discovery of the joys of perspective and point-of-view. First, consider the creation of the world and the Biblical account thereof. The notion of creation has a long history in song and story as well as in

[2]Marshall McLuhan's *The Gutenberg Galaxy* remains important as an extended meditation on this theme.

philosophical, theological, and scientific inquiry, but it is only in the sixteenth century that it was transformed primarily into an "historical" problem: was the Biblical account a scientifically trustworthy and substantially accurate report of the historical event of creation? Jan van Eyck may be thought to show the way into this new thought-world when he vouched for the historical and scientific accuracy of his painting by placing the words "I was here," in the middle of his depiction of the "Arnolfini Betrothal." In the same way, sixteenth century scientists and theologians were able, for the first time, to imagine that the Bible provided something like an eye-witness account of the creation and to treat the sacred text as a visually accurate, and therefore trustworthy, description. Moses could be imagined as the "artist" of creation, and his description of the works of the six days as a personal testimony which, because it described creation from his own point of view and perspective, could be investigated and evaluated just like any other scientific work of art. Moreover, the artist himself was now open to critical historical investigation, and even to the "discovery" that Moses could not have been present at the creation and that his account might therefore be less than fully trustworthy. The question of authority—the authority of Sacred Scripture—was thus historicized. Interest shifted almost imperceptibly in the sixteenth century from a consideration of Moses as the scribe, and God as author of Genesis, to the question of the human author's accuracy and his ability, like Jan van Eyck, to portray the scene of creation in a believable and trustworthy fashion.

It was against this background, of course, that Copernicus, Kepler, and Galileo carried out their famous observations of the stars and planets. Leaving aside the unspoken question of whether they might be better artists of creation than Moses and the Biblical authors, these scholars certainly thought that they could improve on the pictures of creation and of the created world provided by Aristotle, Ptolemy, and the medieval Arabic astronomers. And in fact they could. By setting out with a firm grasp of the scientific principles of visual perspective, they could construct a "world-view"[3] which was more pleasing, more accurate, more true to nature (all of the values prized in contemporary artwork) than that of their predecessors. What might easily pass unnoticed in this achievement, however, are at least two of the unspoken assumptions that made it possible: First, the assumption that there can

[3]The term "world-view" seems to have been a seventeenth-century coinage.

be, as in painting, only one non-erroneous interpretation of the evidence, and that based on the laws of visual perspective and of a determinate point-of-view. Painters knew, of course, that there could be multiple interpretations of the same data—but these were the tricks of perspective which the wary viewer would learn about and avoid. The success of painting rested firmly on the convention that the trained eye can distinguish between "illusion" and "reality," and scientists used the same convention when they began to imagine representing the world "as it really is" (i.e. visually). The second tacit assumption was that Moses, Aristotle, Ptolemy, and all of the medieval scholastics were trying to do the same thing as Copernicus and Kepler and Galileo, that is, to construct a model or a picture of the universe using the science of visual perspective and point-of-view. Because they took this for granted, the scientists of the Baroque period came to historicize the work of their predecessors, and to focus attention not on the realities that the older writers were trying to describe, but rather on those authors' descriptions—that is, on their personal perspective and point-of-view, and on their failure to provide a visually persuasive (i.e. scientific) representation of the motions of the stars and planets.

So successful has been this process of historicization that we are today scarcely able to tell the story differently, to imagine that Moses, Aristotle, and Ptolemy were not at all under the thrall of Renaissance perspective—whose laws had not yet been invented. What might they have been trying to do, if not to provide the kind of picture of reality that we have come to expect from all scientists?[4] What other, and more adequate, ways of understanding their science will allow us to continue to learn about and represent the creation in a fully satisfying way? These are the questions that have emerged in the past few decades as we in the West come gradually out from under the domination of Renaissance perspective and point of view.

A second illustration of the convergence between art and thought may be sought in the history of Jansenism. Cornelius Jansen, a professor at the University of Louvain and then bishop of Ypres, died in 1638, only days after completing the manuscript of his magnum opus, entitled *Augustinus*. This book was the culmination of a lifetime de-

[4]At least until the middle of the twentieth century, when, as in the arts, nonlinear and perspectiveless scientific accounts have once again become imaginable.

voted to reading and study of the voluminous writings of the great fifth–century bishop, Augustine of Hippo. Jansen hoped to find in Augustine the key to overcoming the divisions of the Church, and definitive (i.e. clear and distinct) answers to the great theological questions which were riving her. Jansen's enormous book is, I believe, the first in a long, long line of books on Augustine that attempt to depict in clear and distinct terms the salient aspects of his thought—his personal and authoritative point-of-view on the world and on its Creator and Redeemer.[5] That Jansen's is among the very first of such studies is surely noteworthy; it means that we had to wait more than a thousand years after Augustine's death for our first historical and critical monograph! Surely this is not because preceeding generations had neglected Augustine's writings; that is demonstrably false. Nor were the medieval writers simply too lazy or incompetent to carry out such a study. Rather, it seems, it was only in Jansen's time that one could imagine treating Augustine as a creative artist, and his thought as a consciously crafted work of art in the dominant mode, i.e. with a fixed and personal point of view. In doing so Jansen created something new, "Augustinianism," that is, a coherent doctrine (artistic creation) to rival and to countermand the other "schools of thought," such as Lutheranism, Thomism and Scotism, not to mention Gallicanism and Ultramontanism, which had thrown Europe into such a maelstrom of competing points of view. These other schools had been constructed in the same way, according to the laws and rules of the visual arts which allowed one to distinguish each writer's, or each group's, unique perspective and point of view on key and defining issues.

The success of this intellectual revolution scarcely needs to be emphasized. Its principles and presuppositions have been the touchstones of the entire edifice of higher education into the late twentieth century. The very words "perspective" and "point of view," used to denote an intellectual opinion in almost every undergraduate essay, are witnesses to the success of the artistic metaphor as applied to philosophy, theology and political theory in the Baroque Age. Astonishing as it may seem, there were no corresponding terms to express such an idea in the ancient or medieval world—it was, if we can imagine such a thing, a world without a point of view. Such an assertion is, of

[5]The latest being those published recently by our colleagues, Professors Stock and Rist.

course, difficult to prove, but it is an hypothesis that is well worth testing, and that has important implications for pre- and post-modern intellectual history. If "point-of-view" is a relatively recent innovation rather than an eternal truth about the structure of the universe and of human knowledge, then some of our most cherished beliefs, including our faith in the historical-critical method as the summit of scholarship, are called into question. And such questioning has already begun. Just as the nineteenth century artists gradually came to forego the artful (i.e. artificial) and pleasing certainties of linear perspective and "correct" drawing in order to emphasize other qualities such as solidity, depth, colour, and expressive or symbolic meaning, so too are intellectual historians gradually finding other values to emphasize in their studies of the past. Now, in the last years of the second millenium, historians are nearly ready to sacrifice some of the sophistication and seeming certainty of the historical-critical method. It can now be said in the academy that the "Thomist" and "Scotist" and "Augustinian" points of view, as discovered and codified by the "classical" seventeenth-century interpreters, are chimeras. Soon it may be possible to suggest, for example, that the long-cherished division of early Christian exegesis into Alexandrian (bad) and Antiochene (good) schools of interpretation is equally groundless, being the artificial product of modern intellectual predilections for clear and distinct points of view. Likewise the search for the "historical" Jesus and for the "real" (pre-Justinianic) Roman Law may soon be recognized not as scientific investigations but as the polemical exercises between competing points of view which they are.

Some of this new-found freedom has come to us from the Post-Modern theorists. Foucault and others have pointed toward a new intellectual aesthetic that transcends the old linear ways of thinking. But they, or at least their students, seem not really to have escaped the old model. Theirs seems often to be, rather, a carrying out of the visual logic of the Baroque to one of its possible consequences: that there are multiple points-of-view, and all of them are equally personal and equally in/valid.

As a medievalist I am permitted to be blissfully innocent of all these gambits. I study characters for whom Augustinianism, Neo-Platonism, and Aristotelianism had not yet been invented or "visualized." The ninth century deacon of the Church of Lyons in Southern France, a gentleman by the name of Florus, was every bit as impressed by Augustine as was the seventeenth century Dutchman Cornelius Jansen, and he knew the texts of Augustine equally well. When Florus wanted to harvest the fruits of Augustine's thought he did so not by constructing an historical-critical commentary, but by creating florilegia (collections of flowers—like his name), picking relevant passages from here and there throughout the length and breadth of Augustine's works. These florilegia became the heart of the medieval "gloss" or standard commentary on the Bible. They reflected no single and personal point of view, but rather a common inheritance built up from all the authorities, and in which all readers shared equally.

My own favourite among these pre-moderns is, of course, St. Thomas Aquinas. It is a pleasure, and often a shock for new readers, to watch him invoke the whole gamut of authorities,—from Aristotle to Augustine to the famous Dionysius the Areopagite; the Greek Fathers as well as the Latins; the disciples of Plato as well as the Moslem commentators on Aristotle, all to support in their respective ways the truth of the Christian faith. This is not, of course, the Aquinas of the Baroque or, by and large, of the modern Age. The Thomas of the Baroque was an intellectual genius because he had a particular, Aristotelian, point of view on the cosmos. Viewing everything through the peephole of that perspective, this Pseudo-Thomas could distinguish clearly and distinctly the crucial elements and errors and false perspectives of other authors, and thus refute them.

The real Thomas Aquinas was able to write and think as he did precisely because he had no point of view—he was not an Aristotelian—or even a Thomist. If he were asked, he would surely describe his point of view as that which was common to all Christians in all places and at all times: *Quod semper, ubique, ab omnibus credendum est.* Such a condition was the ordinary one for most people before the Baroque, when opinions (*doxa*) ceased, for a time, to be common (*orthodoxa*) and became instead the expression of particular and personal points-of-view.

Works Cited

Gombrich, Ernst Hans. *The Story of Art.* New York: Phaidon and Oxford UP, 1951 183.

Gombrich, Ernst Hans. *Art and Illusion: A Study in the Psychology of Pictorial Representation.* London: Phaidon, 1972.

McLuhan, Marshall. The Gutenberg Galaxy: The Making of Typographic Man. Toronto: U of Toronto P, 1962.

Eric McLuhan

Francis Bacon's Theory of Communication

ABSTRACT. For centuries, Francis Bacon has been revered as a philosopher and the founder of modern science—an honour which would have baffled him. He thought of himself as a Grammarian, not a Dialectician (Philosopher), and he was engaged in restoring the widom of the ancients, not in founding scientific novelty. The "Novum" in the title of his major work, the Novum Organon (or Novum Organum), was ironic and indicated both that it was intended to supercede the Dialectical Organon of Aristotle and that the work was in support of traditional learning and technique in reading the Book of Nature. In part one, he sets forth his theory of the bias of communication in the famous doctrine of the Idols; in part two, he provides his theory of communication in detail—a theory already present in other works such as the New Atlantis and the Advancement of Learning.

Francis Bacon's theory of communication and of media permeates his work. Often called the father of modern scientific method, Bacon saw his mission as that of restoring in his time the wisdom of the ancients—his program called the Great Instauration.

As a grammarian, Bacon could claim all of human knowledge as his province: *Of The Advancement of Learning* is an encyclopedic report on the state of the arts and sciences in his day. Bacon never for a minute ceases to view the business of the arts and sciences as being the relief of man's fallen moral state (see *Advancement of Learning*, Everyman edition, 37, 138; and *Novum Organum* I, lxviii; xciii; II, lii.). In this matter he is in perfect accord with St. Bonaventure, his ancestor, Roger Bacon, and a long tradition in which man's task had been defined as "as the organization of our earthly exile into a sort of suburb of the heavenly kingdom..." (Etienne Gilson, *The Philosophy of St. Bonaventure* 479). Consequently, Bacon's protestations of

Going for Baroque: Cultural Transformations1550-1650.
A St. Michael's College Symposium. Francesco Guardiani ed. Ottawa: Legas, 1999

originality are seldom to be taken seriously. His account of philosophy in Book I of the *Novum Organum* (lxiii - lxxxviii) is nearly identical with Cicero's. Nor is this strange, since both held the view that the arts are entirely to be judged on the basis of their usefulness to man.

The Grand Renaissance was, in the matter of the revival of grammar, as the method both of science and of theology, not fully achieved until the sixteenth century. Erasmus' great work was to restore patristic theology—that is, grammatical theology. His significance in his own eyes, as well as in the eyes of his age, was that of the man who cast out the stream-lined grammars of the dialecticians of the schools and who restored the full discipline as understood by St. Jerome, the pupil of the great Donatus. "Humanism" was thus for Colet, More, Erasmus, a deliberate return to the Fathers. But that which equally marks the modern Renaissance and lends to it a character which has been much misunderstood is its "science." From the time of the neo-Platonists and Augustine to Bonaventura and to Francis Bacon, the world was viewed as a book, the lost language of which was analogous to that of human speech. Thus the art of grammar provided the sixteenth-century approach not only to the Book of Life in scriptural exegesis but to the Book of Nature, as well.

> Omnis mundi creatura
> Quasi liber et pictura
> Nobis est, et speculum...

The Theory of Words and Scientific Study

In the dialogue named for Cratylus, the follower of Heraclitus, Plato has this exchange between Socrates and Cratylus:

> *Socrates*: But if these things are only to be known through names, how can we suppose that the givers of names had knowledge, or were legislators before there were names at all, and therefore before they could have known them?
> *Cratylus*: I believe, Socrates, the true account of the matter to be, that a power more than human gave things their first names, and that the names which were thus given are necessarily their true names. (Jowett, B. *The Dialogues of Plato*. 4 Vols. New York: Charles Scribners, 1895. Vol. 1, 678.)

Obviously, with this kind of importance associated with the names of things, and of gods, heroes, and legendary beings, etymology would be a main source of scientific and moral enlightenment. And such was the case. The prolific labors of the etymologists reflected in Plato's *Cratylus*, but begun centuries before and continued until the seventeenth century, are as much the concern of the historian of philosophy and of science as of the historian of letters and culture. Indeed, it was not only in antiquity but until the Cartesian revolution that language was viewed as simultaneously linking and harmonizing all the intellectual and physical functions of man and of the physical world as well.

At any time from Plato to Francis Bacon the statement of *Cratylus* would have made sense, and would have evoked respect even when its wider implications were rejected. With the opening of the Christian era, the doctrine of *Cratylus* gained new significance from scriptural exegesis, and especially from *Genesis* 2.19:

> And out of the ground the Lord God formed every beast of the field, and every fowl of the air; and brought them unto the man to see what he would call them: and whatsoever he called every living creature, that was the name thereof.

The doctrine of names is, of course, the doctrine of essence and not a naïve notion of oral terminology.

The scriptural exegetists will hold, as Francis Bacon held, that Adam possessed metaphysical knowledge in a very high degree. To him the whole of nature was a book which he could read with ease. He lost this ability to read this language as a result of his fall; and Solomon alone of the sons of men has ever recovered the power to read the book of nature. The business of art is, however, to recover the knowledge of that language which once man held by nature. The problem as to which of the arts should have priority in the work of explaining man and nature had arisen among the pre-Socratics. Grammar, or allegorical exegesis of natural phenomena, as well as of folk myths and even the works of Homer and Hesiod, enjoyed many advantages for the task. In the Cratylus, however, Plato asserts the superior claims of dialectics for the same work, but, as a philosopher who habitually employed the grammatical modes of poetry and myth to express his own most significant and esoteric teaching, he is far from confident that grammar can be or ought to be entirely superseded. Shortly afterwards, however, Aristotle established the nature of non-grammatical scientific method in the Posterior Analytics. His achievement bore no fruit until the twelfth century. Until the twelfth century, therefore, grammar reigned unrivalled as the prime mode of science, and, from the patristic period, of theology as well. But grammar was far from forgotten during the great age of dialectics. In the thirteenth century, with the triumph of Aristotle in St. Thomas Aquinas, came simultaneously the consummate achievement of the grammatical method in St. Bonaventura. (The great grammarians are also alchemists.) There is thus not the least incongruity in the fact that eminent humanists like Pico Della Mirandola and Cornelius Agrippa are also alchemists. The grammatical method in science, therefore, persists as long as alchemy, which is to say, well into the eighteenth century. But from the time of Descartes the main mode of science is, of course, mathematical. In our own time the methods of anthropology and psychology have re-established grammar as, at least, a valid mode of science.

Needless to say, Aristotle did not share the analogist's view of words and phenomena as interrelated by proportions and etymologies. Yet, dialectics and rhetoric in the hands of the analogists were certainly refashioned until they became not merely sciences but the queens of the sciences. This is true not merely of Ciceronian rhetoric and scholastic dialectics, but of the "system" of Francis Bacon as well. (*Advancement* 66.)

At the core of his program, Bacon puts the traditional role of the arts as providing the indispensable training for the sciences: "Our labours must therefore be directed towards inquiring into and observing resemblances and analogies, both in the whole and in its parts, for they unite nature, and lay the foundation of the sciences." (*Novum Organum* II, xxvii) And at the close of the *Novum Organum* Bacon points out that it "springs from the nature of things, as well as from that of the mind," and that much care must be expended in perceptual training and practical modes of criticism and observation, either to "assist and cure the understanding and senses, or furnish our general practice" (II, lii).

Idols and the Bias of Perception

Naturally, Bacon turned his attention to bias and corruption on the faculties and as imposed by media:

> [T]he powers of bodies are more or less impeded or advanced by the medium, according to the nature of the bodies and their effective powers, and also according to that of the medium. For one medium is adapted to light, another to sound, another to heat and cold, another to magnetic action, and so on. (*Novum Organum* II, xlviii)

He mounted a two-pronged counterattack on the bias of communication. First, he identified the "false gods" or idols which bewitch and confuse human reason (weakened by the Fall), so that once seen they might be purged. Second, he prescribed a means of re-engaging and retuning the faculties by writing in aphoristic style. As early as the Advancement of Learning the Idols appear in embryo:

> But lastly there is a much more important and profound kind of fallacies in the mind of man which I find not observed or inquired at all, and think good to place here, as that which of all others appertaineth most to rectify judgment: the force whereof is such, as it doth not dazzle or snare the understanding in some particulars, but doth more generally and inwardly infect and corrupt the state thereof. For the mind of man is far from the nature of a clear and equal glass, wherein the beams of things should reflect according to their true incidence; nay, it is rather like an enchanted glass, full of superstition and imposture, if it be not delivered and reduced. For this purpose, let us consider the false appearances that are imposed upon us be the general nature of the mind. (*Advancement* 132. Cf. also "Idols of the Tribe," *Novum Organum* I, xxiv-xxxi)

> Let us consider again the false appearances imposed upon us by every man's own individual nature and custom. (*Advancement* 134. Cf. also "Idols of the Cave," *Novum Organum* I, xxxi-xxxv)

> And lastly let us consider the false appearances that are imposed upon us by words, which are framed and applied according to the conceit and capacities of the vulgar sort: and although we think we govern our words, and prescribe it well, loquendum ut vulgus, sentiendum ut sapientes; yet certain it is that words, as a Tartar's bow, do shoot back upon the understanding of the wisest, and mightily entangle and pervert the judgment. (*Advancement* 134)

> Tantum series juncturaque pollet,
> Tantum de medio sumptis accedit honoris;
> —Hor. Ep. Ad Pis. 242
>
> as a man shall make a great shew of an art, which, if it were disjointed, would come to little. Secondly, methods are more fit to win consent or belief, but less fit to point to action; for they carry a kind of demonstration in orb or circle, one part illuminating another, and therefore satisfy; but particulars, being dispersed, do best agree with dispersed directions. And lastly, Aphorisms, representing a knowledge broken, do invite men to inquire further; whereas Methods, carrying the show of a total, do secure men, as if they were at farthest. (*Advancement* 142)

Knowledge in discontinuous form has specific power to involve:

> ...for the contemplation of God's creatures and works produceth (having regard to the works and creatures themselves) knowledge, but having regard to God, no perfect knowledge but wonder, which is broken knowledge. (Advancement, Everyman, page 7)

Using the traditional awareness of the impact of style on the perceptions of the audience, Bacon saw his *Novum Organum*, for example as remedial: the choice of aphoristic style was calculated to freshen awareness and assist in purging the bias of communication. Mind and senses had to be cleansed to prepare them for the great task of reading and interpreting the Two Books.

Formal Cause and the Encyclopedia of Knowledge

As much as literature, Nature is an encyclopedia, so the grammarian needed full knowledge of the trivium and quadrivium as well as keen perception and critical faculties. The objective of using the arts and sciences to penetrate the Book of Nature is ever to recover knowledge of the languages in which it is inscribed, lost at the Fall. To this task grammar brings all of its tools of interpretation and etymology and formal analysis. Bacon opens Book II of the *Novum Organum* with a report on the state of understanding in each of the four departments of causality.

> The unhappy state of man's actual knowledge is manifest . . . It is rightly laid down that true knowledge is that which is deduced from causes. The division of four causes also is not amiss: matter, form, the efficient, and end or final cause. Of these, however, the latter is so far from being beneficial, that it even corrupts the sciences . . . The discovery of form is considered desperate. As for the efficient cause and matter . . . they are but desultory and superficial, and of scarcely any avail to real and active knowledge.

The discovery of form united all labours on the Two Books; for, as held throughout the tradition, the forms manifest the Logos and provide the common language in which both Books are inscribed. They serve not as the figure but the ground of matter, and they underlie the analogical ratios between the Two Books. In this regard, etymology provides a major technique of scientific investigation. The whole aim of the arts and sciences therefore is to enable the discovery and understanding, and ultimately the manipulation (alchemy), of forms. This constitutes media study of a high order. The great alchemists, the Paracelsans from Raymond Lully to Cornelius Agrippa, were grammarians. Bacon is perfectly aware of how the sciences and arts are united by the study of forms and formal causes:

> On a given basis of matter to impose any nature, within the limits of possibility, is the intention of human power. In like manner, to know the causes of a given effect, in whatever subject, is the intention of human knowledge: which intentions coincide. For that which is in contemplation as a cause, is in operation as a medium....
>
> He who knows the efficient and materiate causes, composes or divides things previously invented, or transfers and produces them; also in matter somewhat similar, he attaineth unto new inventions; the more deeply fixed limits of things he moveth not.
>
> He who knows the forms, discloses and educes things which have not hitherto been done, such as neither the vicissitudes of nature, nor the diligence of experience might ever have brought into action, or as might not have entered into man's thoughts. (—Tract entitled "Francis Bacon's Aphorisms and Advices Concerning the Helps of the Mind and the Kindling of Natural Light")

Francis Bacon's theory of communication, then, has these two main elements. For one, there is the conventional understanding of the analogical relation of the Two Books and the entire tradition of words and of forms that surrounds it. For the second, his view of the mind as prey to Idolatry of various kinds since it was weakened by the Fall—false perception and skewed judgment—and in need of remedy. His solution to these include identifying and clearing away of Idols and the employment of aphorisms to reengage the faculties and restore their acuity and wonder.

Just as Bacon was later to claim in attacking the dialecticians, St. Augustine says arts and knowledge are for use, for the relief of man's estate; and, as Bacon freely admits, the greatest art is theology, since it is for the relief of man's spiritual estate.

> But the greatest error of all the rest is the mistaking or misplacing of the last or farthest end of knowledge: for men have entered into a desire of learning and knowledge, sometimes upon a natural curiosity and inquisitive appetite; sometimes to entertain their minds with variety and delight; sometimes for ornament and reputation; and sometimes to enable them to victory of wit and contradiction; and most times for lucre and profession; and seldom sincerely to give a true account of their gift of reason, to the benefit and use of men: as if there were sought in knowledge a couch whereupon to rest a searching and restless spirit; or a tarrasse, for a wandering and variable mind to walk up and down with a fair prospect; or a tower of state for a proud mind to raise itself upon; or a fort or commanding ground, for strife and contention; or a shop, for profit or sale; and not a rich storehouse, for the glory of the Creator and the relief of man's estate. (*Advancement* 34-35).

Domenico Pietropaolo

Galileo's Concept of Biblical Allegory and the Baroque Vision of Reality

ABSTRACT. My purpose in this paper is to examine Galileo's concept of allegory as a hermeneutical tool, viewed against the background of the allegorical tradition and appraised in the context of the relationship between physics and theology presupposed by his scientific research. My method will be to focus on Galileo's most significant allusions to allegory, to sort out the chief issues involved in an analysis of the idea of allegory that they presuppose, and finally to correlate the logical, aesthetic, theological, and physical implications of that idea with his vision of reality as a scientist, all in the context of the baroque perspective on the representation of immanence and transcendence.

In a letter dated 23 March 1615 and addressed to Monsignor Piero Dini, Galileo very succinctly described the troubled relationship between physics and theology by comparing the tension between them to the discordant sound produced by strings vibrating out of tune, and by suggesting that the dissonance could not be resolved until such time as the two disciplines were brought into a dialogue of mutual enlightenment: you cannot tune two strings, he said, by listening to only one of them.[1] Rooted at once in his father's experiments on harmonic modulation and in the contemporary Baroque predilection for a rhetoric capable of using the human sensorium as a channel to transcendence, the metaphor of discordant tones is a powerful and complex allegory in which Revelation is figured as music, the Bible and

[1] Galilei, "A Monsignor Piero Dini": " Quando si abbino a concordar luoghi sacri con dottrine naturali nuove e non comuni, è necessario avere intera notizia di tal dottrine, non si potendo accordar due corde insieme col sentirne una sola" (73). For an English translation, see *The Galileo Affair* (63).

Going for Baroque: Cultural Transformations1550-1650.
A St. Michael's College Symposium. Francesco Guardiani ed. Ottawa: Legas, 1999

the same claim, Galileo was on safe ground, since Dante's statement was itself an echo of words written by St. Thomas at the very beginning of the *Summa Theologica*.[8] However the use that he makes of the passage is quite different. Both St Thomas and Dante stress that in Scripture anthropomorphic figurative language is an aid to understanding, an instrument through which its sense becomes easier to grasp, given that our powers of comprehension cannot soar to pure intellection other than by way of the senses. "So must one speak to imperfection ," says Beatrice to Dante, in Ciardi's translation of the *Paradiso*, "which only from the *sensible* apprehends / whatever it then makes fit for intellection. / Scripture in like manner condescends / describing God as having hands and feet / as signs to men of what more it portends." St Thomas had said the same thing, though he assumed that corporeal imagery was used in the Bible for the benefit of those who need material analogies in order to conceive spiritual truths: "It is befitting Holy Writ ... that spiritual truths be expounded by means of figures taken from corporeal things, in order that thereby even the simple who are unable by themselves to grasp intellectual things may be able to understand it." By understanding the figurative language, readers of the Bible would be enabled to understand its sense. Whether the simple are some, as for St. Thomas, or all of mankind, as for Dante, there is no question that for both the intent behind the allegorical language of the Bible is to facilitate intellection of transcendence by way of material reality.

At the level of pure cognition, the surface sense of the corporeal narrative is related to the intended one by continuity and progression, in accordance with a dynamic of consciousness determined by the hierarchical scheme of things that obtained prior to the Copernican revolution. Rhetorically, the figure by which this type of relationship is best expressed is synecdoche, a figure that leads the mind to the whole by showing to it one of its parts. In the Ptolemaic world, synecdoche had a metaphysical sweep that it would never have again.

Divina Commedia, testo critico stabilito da Giorgio Petrocchi. The English translation quoted below is from *The Paradiso*, trans. John Ciardi.

[8] "Convenit etiam sacrae Scripturae...ut spirtualia sub similitudinibus corporalium proponantur, ut saltem vel sic rudes eam capiant, qui ad intelligibilia ecundum se capienda non sunt idonei" *Summa theologica,* I, q. 1, a. 9, resp.

It is a figure that describes the structure of the universe and that of its human apprehension before the advent of the heliocentric system. As a system of concentric spheres in which the smaller ones are the content of the larger ones, in a geometric ascension from the earth to the primum mobile, the Ptolemaic universe has a clear synecdochical structure. Moreover, synecdoche describes the structure of all categorical knowledge, since definition itself is based on participation by inclusion in successively larger concepts, as when we say that Peter is a man, that a man is a rational being, that a rational being is a living being, and so on ascending up to being itself, as the final end of the process of reasoning; it also describes the structure of syllogistic logic, since the conclusion of an argument, as the deduction that Socrates is mortal, is only a clarification of the fact that the entity that it names is but an element of the class of entities given in the major premise, as in the statement that all men are mortal.[9] And just as synecdoche permits us to ascend slowly from unity to infinity, so it enables the reader to rise from the surface rhetoric of the text to the ultimate meaning that lies high above it, from the concrete signs that are easy to grasp to the transcendent meaning that they really "portend."

Not so for Galileo, who, almost imperceptibly, turns the sense of the passage in a different direction and then argues from it, as if from a theory of unbridgeable semantic discontinuity between surface and intended meanings, an idea on which the most widespread classical and post-medieval concepts of allegory are hinged, for an allegorical reading of the passages in the Bible in which there are apparently incorrect references to the behaviour of nature. In his view the recourse to surface narratives based on common sense and on an unreflective perception of the world reveals on the part of the sacred authors the awareness that some ideas, be they of a metaphysical or of a physical nature, cannot be grasped by novices and simple folk, though they can be fully understood by initiates and men of superior intelligence and training. The representation of things, not as they really are, but as they appear to be to the common man, is the result of a rhetorical

[9] Coleridge would later make this idea the basis of his ontological and rhetorical theory of symbol, which sees the cosmos as "definitionally synechdochic," as John A. Hodgson observes in "Transcendental Tropes: Coleridge's Rhetoric of Allegory and Symbol" (275).

strategy designed to produce a text capable of being intellectually satisfying to both groups, simple readers being allowed to fix their gaze onto the opacity of the surface while their more sophisticated counterparts are invited to penetrate the surface and to leap into the world of ideas located somewhere outside the text, in the realm of the disciplines which constitute the higher forms of knowledge and to which the surface narrative bears no necessary resemblance. But even such highly qualified readers require guidance when they cross the boundaries of their fields of expertise, and that is why rigorous theological exegesis of the biblical text is necessary.

Ironically, exegetical commentaries of this kind are of benefit only to readers well equipped to understand the higher truths contained in the text. For the "few" who deserve to be distinguished from the common herd, Galileo observes, "it is necessary that wise interpreters produce their true meaning and indicate the particular reasons why they have been expressed by [*profferiti sotto*] such words." (p. 50)[10]. The clause "expressed by such words", used by the English translator, is a somewhat inadequate rendition of the original text, in which Galileo says expressed *under* such words, clearly implying an intention on the part of the Biblical authors to conceal the more recondite ideas from the masses, an intention borne out by other passages in the letter to Christina, where Galileo speaks explicitly of deliberately hidden meanings.[11] When this nuance is returned to the text, and with it the suggestion that, like an ordinary poet, the Holy Ghost has occasionally preferred the rhetoric of concealment to that of openness, the episode becomes at once very significant. For, in the first place, what we have here is, not an epistemological synecdoche linking one cognitive entity to the other, but a marked discontinuity between the se-

[10] "Così per quei pochi che meritano d'esser separati dalla plebe è necessarioche i saggi espositori produchino i veri sensi, e n'additino le ragioni particolari per che siano sotto cotali parole stati profferiti" (48).

[11] For example: "For the sole purpose of accommodating popular understanding the Scripture has not abstained from concealing the most important truths, attributing to God characteristics that are contrary to or even very far from his essence" (Finocchiaro 92); "it is appropriate for Scripture to say many things that are different in appearance and in regard to the literal meaning of the words) from the absolute truth" (*Ibid.* 93).

mantic domain of the surface, where the masses contentedly come to rest, and that of the realm of ideas beneath it, available only to the superior minds who make bold use of their native genius to cross the boundary of appearances and to venture with confidence into the ocean of profound thought that lies beyond it. What is more, this semantic domain, in perfect consonance with the Baroque vision of reality, is not represented by resemblance and inclusion, as a microcosm may be said to represent by resemblance the macrocosm that includes it, or as an antitype the type that fulfils it, and, more generally, as the language of all texts, with its imagery, rhythms, and structures, the world that it describes, but by things that have no apparent relation to it other than the fictional one that is required by the act of interpretation. Henceforth, observes Foucault, things and words "were to be separated from one another" (43).

Moreover this domain is reserved for a small aristocracy of readers. There is no sense that the masses, weighed down as they are by the burden of their ignorance and by the grossness of their intellects (*vulgo assai rozo e indisciplinato, p. 89)*, can ever reach it, whatever their disposition. Their passive and unreflective perception of the scheme of things shackles them to the surface of the text. It is not for their benefit but for the further edification of already enlightened minds, for those "who deserve to be distinguished from the plebeians" (p. 89, trans. mine), that the theologians must labour in their efforts to explain the more recondite truths in Holy Scripture. Why is it, Galileo asks, no doubt grounding his question in the dialectic between exoteric and esoteric pedagogy which Christian hermeneutics, chiefly by way of Origen, had inherited from Greek humanism,[12] that the Holy Spirit "has sometimes wanted to hide them under words with a different literal meaning" (p.105)? This is the question that must properly guide biblical exegesis.

What we have here is a classic description of the concept of allegory, understood rhetorically as a way of constructing a text with a double focus, one near and the other far, metaphysically as a device for expressing the discrete nature of reality, sociologically as a means for speaking simultaneously to groups with a different capacity to understand and appreciate uncommon ideas, and politically as a form of communication that privileges an aristocracy of cultured readers,

[12] See, for example, Werner Jaeger, *Early Christianity and Greek Paideia*, chapter 5.

each already in possession of some aspect of the truth and each now ready to be tutored in the reasoning of God. In this conception of allegory, which has almost nothing in common with the one that obtained prior to the Copernican revolution, and which, especially in its typological mode, was still practised by Galileo's more orthodox contemporaries,[13] the key presupposition is that the structure of reality cannot be described by the rhetoric of synecdoche and resemblance. Whereas in the medieval and Renaissance cosmos each sphere and each genus could be regarded as a synecdoche of the sphere and genus which included it as part of its content in the next order of magnitude, and of which they might be taken as signs in virtue of the resemblance that linked them to each other and both to the ground-plan of creation, so that through one object, made, as it were, transparent by the system, one could see the other and through the other the totality, in the Baroque world of post-Copernican astronomy, when the spheres had been dissolved away into nothingness, when verticality was flattened out and celestial science was reduced to terrestrial physics, all objects of perception became totally opaque while resemblance of attributes proved to be a fraudulent guide to the discovery of shared metaphysical essence.

The loss of transparency and resemblance anchored the Baroque world-view to physical reality and made available to art the possibility of using any object to represent any other with which it may or may not share a metaphysical base, privileging metaphor and allegory as never before in history. The physical structure of the world and the metaphysical order that could be inferred from it were not centred on man and were not constructed on the axis of his return journey to God, but on nature. When art focused its gaze on the materiality of nature, it noticed with unprecedented clarity and breadth of vision its infinite richness, its interior multiplicity, its dizzying dynamism, its drama, its countless internal transformations, its echoes and mirages, resulting from the deceptive nature of resemblance—all thematic headings under which much of the poetry and many of the paintings of the time can be grouped—and it discovered what exploratory power there could be in the rhetoric of mere description and substitu-

[13] The playwright Federico della Valle, for example, on whose typological interpretation of the Book of Judith see my essay "Iudit, *femme fatale* of the Baroque Stage."

tion. Baroque man, too, of course, had a strong yearning for the infinite, but in expressing it, he never left the realm that was available to him only through his senses. Anchored as it was to the material world, his imagination could not lead him progressively out of it to transcendence. Fantasy, as Husserl observed in his essay on Galileo, "can transform sensible shapes only into other sensible shapes"(25).[14] The Baroque imagination does not take leave of nature in order to know the spiritual but thinks the spiritual by means of and within the flesh. The experience of infinity that it yearns for, and in which it finds satisfaction, is the experience of something that in the end turns out to be immanent in the materiality of nature, the Baroque vision being one of the materialisation of spirit rather than of the spiritualisation of matter. The human senses are, as it were, stretched out until, through them, the imagination gives body and shape to the human experience of spirit. As a result, as Wylie Sypher stated in a truly significant observation, "thought does really become a physical experience" (65).[15]

In this vision of reality, the scientist occupies a place of great privilege, since it is science, rather than theology or metaphysics, that determines the dimensions, shape and content of the picture. The sociological and political aspects of the concept of allegory presupposed by Galileo are a consequence of the coming into prominence of science, rising to authority next to theology rather than within it. The Baroque book of nature was the domain of science, and the mode of reading that it required differed immeasurably from the mode of reading that Galileo could recommend for the Bible. Unlike language, understood in its most general acceptation of means of expression and communication, nature cannot lie. In the book of nature, there cannot be any allegories, because none of its objects could be regarded as only a sign for an object located somewhere beyond its domain. The

[14] David Carr, translator of *The Crisis of European Sciences and Transcendental Phenomenology*, suggests that Husserl added the essay on "Galileo's Mathematization of Nature" to the initial redaction of the *Crisis* after a visit from his former student and distinguished Galileo scholar Alexander Koyré (p. xix).

[15] From Wylie Sypher's *Four Stages of Renaissance Style,* as cited by Harold B. Segel in *The Baroque Poem.*

book of nature speaks of nature, of the sense that is immanent in it, and of nothing else. The alphabet in which it is written, says Galileo in what is perhaps the most famous passage in all of his works, consists of geometrical figures, and so geometry is the code that the scientist in his experience of nature must use in order to decipher its content and hence to discover the laws that God, in the act of creation, ordained that it should obey in order for it to be what it is.[16] Once they have been discovered, the laws of nature must then be used as guide by anyone making any statements, however incidentally, about nature in the context of all other disciplines and in the interpretation of written texts, including the Bible, which contain references to natural phenomena. Biblical exegesis must seek orientation from science in annotating all references to the material world. And if it should find that the sacred text includes statements contrary to established science, it will know for certain that in those passages the text is speaking allegorically, and so it must provide a reading that will explain away the difference and, what is more, identify the reasons why the Holy Ghost in those instances induced the sacred authors to conceal the truth under an allegorical narrative of popular misconceptions. If exegesis does all that, it will offer an interpretation of the Bible which will not force the text to say what it never was intended to say.

At that point, and only at that point, will the Baroque allegory of a culture shaped by disciplines that stand comfortably in each other's

[16]And just as the language of a text is by no means identical with its essence, geometry is not identical with the essence of nature, in a Platonic sense. The view taken here is that Galileo's mathematisation of nature is no more than an interpretation of its phenomena which uses mathematics as an aid. The thesis that Galileo was ultimately concerned only with mathematical essences rather than scientific procedures was championed by Alexandre Koyrê, who interpreted his scientific work as a Platonic and medievalising reaction to Aristotelianism. The instrumental role of mathematics in Galileo has been stressed instead by Ludovico Geymonat and, among others, by Stillman Drake in his *Galileo at Work*, a biography that, as the title implies, shows Galileo as a working scientist rather than as a Platonic philosopher contemplating mathematical essences. In a later essay, based on Galileo's manuscript notes, "Galileo and Mathematical Physics," Drake states that the idea "that space and time could be identified with mathematical entities, which became popular early in this century, entailed in the seventeenth century an absurdity, the confusion of a thing with its measure"(640).

debt and that contribute willingly to each other's enlightenment, an allegory so effectively textualised as the pithy narrative of two performers adjusting their strings so that their joint vibrations may carry forth the truth of existence, finally indicate something within human reach. That desideratum was not, as the trial of Galileo made all too clear, within the possibilities of the seventeenth century, and the debate, though not on the astronomical front, occasionally flares up even in our own cynical times–though the scientists of our generation, more keenly aware then their Baroque predecessors could ever be of the extent to which the technical disciplines can thrive in isolation from metaphysical discussions, tend to work, for better or worse, at a respectful distance from the disciplines concerned with the scheme of things in its totality. Now that the long period we call the age of modernity, which began more or less in the troubled years of the early Baroque, is over, according to some, or going through its last difficult moments, according to others, our culture approaches with suspicion anyone who claims to speak with authority in virtue of some special anointing, religious or secular though its source may be, and, consequently, encourages isolation and measures the progress of each discipline without making significant reference to that of the others. However, history does not really consist of separate streams flowing independently in parallel directions, but of one single river moving into the future, as we inevitably realise whenever scientific research agitates questions of vast ethical magnitude. The memory of Galileo's experience then looms large, and we are taught, again and again, that no significant progress can take place until we are able to conceive of a culture in which each discipline is moved by the obligation to build on the achievements of the others.

WORKS CITED

Alighieri, Dante. *La Divina Commedia*. Ed. Giorgio Petrocchi. Torino: Einaudi, 1975.

__________. *The Paradiso*. Trans. John Ciardi. New York: Mentor, 1970.

Argan, Carlo Giulio. "La retorica e l'arte barocca." Id., *Studi e note dal Bramante al Canova*. Roma: Bulzoni, 1970. 167-176.

__________. "Retorica e architettura." Id., *Studi e note dal Bramante al Canova.* Roma: Bulzoni, 1970. 177-184.

Drake, Stillman. "Galileo and Mathematical Physics." *Scienza e filosofia: Saggi in onore di Ludovico Geymonat.* Milano: Garzanti, 1985.

__________. *Galileo at Work.* Chicago: U of Chicago P, 1978.

Foucault, Michel. *The order of things: An Archaeology of the Human Sciences.* New York: Random House, 1970.

Galilei, Galileo. "A Monsignor Piero Dini." *Sulla libertà della scienza e l'autorità delle scritture.* Ed. Maddalena Montinari. Roma: Theoria, 1983

__________. *Considerazioni al Tasso.* In *Scritti letterari.* Ed. Alberto Chiari. Firenze: Le Monnier, 1943

__________. *The Galileo Affair: A Documentary History*, edited and translated with an introduction and notes by Maurice A. Finocchiaro. Berkeley: U of California P, 1989.

Geymonat, Ludovico *Galileo Galilei.* Torino: Einaudi, 1965.

Hodgs, John A. "Transcendental Tropes: Coleridge's rhetoric of Allegory and Symbol." *Allegory, Myth and Symbol.* Ed. M.W. Bloomfield. Cambridge, Mass.: Harvard UP, 1981.

Husserl, Edmund .*The Crisis of European Sciences and Transcendental Phenomenology.* Trans. David Carr. Evanston: Northwestern UP, 1970.

Jaeger, Werner. *Early Christianity and Greek Paideia.* Cambridge, Mass.: Harvard UP, 1961.

John Paul II. "Message to the Pontifical Academy of Sciences." *The Quarterly Review of Biology* 72.4(1997): 382.

Koyré, Alexandre. *Etudes Galiléennes.* Paris: Hermann, 1939.

Lamberton, Robert. *Homer the Theologian.* Berkeley: Uof California P, 1986),

Panofsky, Erwin. *Galileo as a Critic of the Arts.* The Hague: Martinus Nijhoff, 1954.

Pietropaolo, Domenico. "Iudit, *femme fatale* of the Baroque Stage," *Donna.* Ed. Ada Testaferri. Ottawa: Dovehouse, 1989. 273-283.

Segel, Harold B. *The Baroque Poem.* New York: Dutton, 1974.

Sypher, Wylie. *Four Stages of Renaissance Style.* New York: Garden City, 1955.

Weinberg, Bernard. *A History of Literary Criticism in the Italian Renaissance.* Chicago: U of Chicago P, 1961.

Francesco Guardiani

Baroque and Neobaroque

ABSTRACT. I view Baroque as a cultural interface of epochal dimension set between the old and the new, the old aural world of manuscript culture and the new world of print that was "rolling off the press." Today, as we move away from the "modern" mechanism of print to the "post-modern" circuitry of electronics, we find ourselves immersed in a similarly patterned, highly creative and equally unstable, hybrid cultural condition that we may call Neobaroque.

To begin, here and now. There are times, in the life of a man (or in the life of a woman, *ça va sans dire*), when one feels the need to stop, look around, retrace his own steps, consider how he got where he is. It might happen in the middle of a city never visited before, or perhaps while driving in a highway with too many or not enough signs. There and then one has to come up with an assessment of the situation, and decide what to do next.

I think we live in a particular historical period that demands this kind of assessment. We simply do not see a linear "development" (to use an obsolete term) of our present condition. Rather, we perceive that we are in the eye of an epochal storm, in the middle of a gigantic transformation that can take us (before taking our children) anywhere, in terms of cultural as well as socio-economic conditions.

Once we stop where we are, to reflect on how we got here, the first obstacle we encounter, for a clear vision of the present as well as the past, is our own culturally conditioned view. Our culture works as a filter that "colours" every perception; in that, it is an obstacle, no doubt. But our culture is also our home, and we would be even more lost without it. And so, we must become aware and flexible. Aware of our limited, or filtered view, and flexible in adapting our logic inside and outside of our cultural home.

With our flexible approach, an obvious, but problematic opening statement for an analysis of the present would be: "We are now living in the middle of a crisis." This implies a precedent condition of not crisis;

Going for Baroque: Cultural Transformations1550-1650.
A St. Michael's College Symposium. Francesco Guardiani ed. Ottawa: Legas, 1999

and since nobody likes crisis, and the precedent condition would be better than the one we are immersed in, we would also consider ourselves afflicted by a sense of anxiety and with a desire to get out of this sick state, get out of this crisis, as soon as possible. Continuing with our "we are in a crisis scenario" we would have to analyze the crisis, without forgetting that we are immersed in it..., before deciding what to do, where to turn.

For a more relaxed view of the present we should perhaps erase every negative connotation from the word "crisis," but since that is hardly possible, we could perhaps speak of our present condition as "a period of accelerated cultural transformation." The definition gives us a good point of departure, a more solid, albeit in motion, term of reference without moralizing, or de-moralizing connotations. After all, we want to understand where we are and that assessment has to be as neutral as possible.

And so we observe our reality. It is made of instability, of discontinuous, fragmentary and episodic artistic and literary discourses as it is of heuristic and... *feeble,* as it has been called, philosophy. It is made of a great tension between an aging materialistic epistemology and a new appreciation of spiritual values. It is also made of unhappiness with heuristic and feeble philosophy, and of new and great "imperial" designs of future epics. And it is made, *in fine,* of a new form of "monarchy" that I would call iconic (with new kings and queens as stars, sports stars, music stars[1], models and supermodels as stars, aristocratic people redefined media stars, like Lady Di, and of course Hollywood "true" stars): a new form monarchy that accompanies the decline of democracy (as we have intended it for most of the modern age, the democracy of the ballot box.

We seem to be, to conclude the preamble, in a moment of extreme tension between the future and the past. We are all aware that changes are inevitable, but at the same time are attached to the reality that we know best, trust and feel that we can control if not dominate.

To make sense of all this, to understand our present cultural condition, our best bet is history. Perhaps we have been here before, perhaps we are in a phase of a cultural cycle that has already been defined in the past. If we could retrace the pattern we would know what is the next phase of the cycle and look at the future with more confidence.

[11] A significant series of aristocratic titles appears in the music world, where we have a king, with Elvis, a Duke (Ellington), and a Prince, followed by a more demotic, equally iconic, re-tribalized Boss (Bruce Springstein).

Is there a sense in history?

Is there a sense in history? is my loose translation of *Se la storia ha un senso*, the title of a recent book by an Italian colleague, Remo Bodei, teaching philosophy at the university of Pisa. There might be a sense but we don't see it anymore, is the implicit answer. Determined to be an optimist in a nihilistic world, Bodei concludes by pointing to a paradoxical advantage: since we do not know where we are going perhaps we are free to choose, or better, to create, establish or project *ex novo* our future destination (if we insist on having one). This solution, or rather this escape from chaos or nothingness, is ingenious but I am afraid it doesn't help us to get out of a general feeling of unredeemable impotence. "There aren't too many people today," Bodei says, "who by reason, rather than by faith, can affirm that history has a sense" (17). Of course, the assumption here is that reason is better than faith. But for our purpose, it could be read differently: it is reason, and not faith, that is struck by a crisis; it is reason, and not faith, that cannot cope with contemporary reality.

An so, perhaps, we can turn somewhere else for help, where there is some faith. Northrop Frye has always fascinated me: often when I am stuck with a problem, missing link in my train of thought, I get the distinct feeling that he has gone through an identical or similar thinking pattern.. but of course he always has the answer. And here it is, from *The Great Code*: a theory of history with faith.

> Typology is a figure of speech that moves in time: the type exists in the past and the antitype in the present, or the type exists in the present and the antitype in the future. What typology really is as a mode of thought, what it both assumes and leads to, is a theory of history, or more accurately of historical process: an assumption that there is meaning and point to history, and that sooner or later some event or events will occur which will indicate what that meaning or point is, and so become an antitype of what has happened previously. Our modern confidence in historical process, our belief that despite apparent confusion, even chaos in human events, nevertheless those events are going somewhere and indicating something, is probably a legacy of Bible typology: at least I can think of no other source for its tradition. (81)

Of course, Frye's "modern confidence in historical process," of which he speaks in 1992, plays havoc with Bodei's end of the century doubts (or end of the second millennium doubts, which for some reason correspond to the end of history as a linear narrative or process), and we are not making collective psychological anxieties go away by announcing an *older* theory. We can work with Frye, however, and see, within the wide scope of historical typology, if we can recognize a phase of *development, becoming or transformation,* that reminds us of our present cultural conditions. We have several choices: different but similar theories of the cyclical flowing of history offer us a view of a particular interest for our purpose. Specifically, we are focusing on the phase (or part of it) that corresponds to the end of a cycle and the beginning of next one.

Skipping the pagan saturnalia or the death and resurrection of Adonis, as well as the apocalyptic design of Gioacchino da Fiore, we could pause at Giambattista Vico's theory of *corsi and ricorsi*. Since it is also part of a reasoned out *Scienza nuova*, or new science of the exclusively man made history and not an article of faith, it might serve to dispel any doubt on the amplest applicability of the theory: not only useful, in other words, to the faithful.

But even with Vico, we have some practical limitations: the development of the nations from the age of the Gods to the age of the heroes, and from this to the age of man, with the corresponding development in the human mind, of the senses, the imagination and the reason, is too large a framework to be reduced to a manageable set of distinctive values for one of its phases.

Vico, thank God, inspired a large number of thinkers, from Heinrich Wölfflin to Hayden White, from Frye to McLuhan, each developing their own system. We can trust Wölfflin with the geometrical 'correction' of the *circular* design of history by Vico with the *spiral*: we return to the beginning of a cycle but not to the identical spot, the shift being a consequence of chronology. The consciousness of a linear, chronological flowing of history, is so much part of our culture, so much part of our understanding of history, that *we have to* make it part of our rational understanding of the present. And we are certainly grateful to Hayden White for making us acutely aware of the *creative* nature of historiography. A good way to look at it, I believe, is to be conscious of making contemporary history as we write about the past, however distant; and this, of course, applies to personal biases as well: as we become aware of the "filtered view" imposed by our cultural environment, we are also sensitive to our own biases. Finally: to be conscious of the impossibility of total objectivity make us humble, aware and flexible, if I can repeat with some theoretical backing the good intention stated at the beginning of this paper. We shall turn now to some of Frye's categories. McLuhan will help us later.

Patterns of archetypal becoming

Frye sets up his historical *modes* right at the beginning of his *Anatomy of Criticism*.

> Fiction [...] may be classified [...] by the hero's power of action, which may be greater than ours, less, or roughly the same. Thus:
> 1. If superior in *kind* both to other men and to the environment of other men, the hero is a divine being, and the story about him will be a *myth* in the common sense of a story about a god. Such story have an important place in literature, but are as a rule found outside the normal literary categories.
> 2. If superior in *degree* to other men and to his environment, the hero is the typical hero of *romance,* whose actions are marvelous but who is himself identified as a human being. [...]
> 3. If superior in degree to other men but not to his natural environment, the hero is a leader. [...] This is the hero of the *high mimetic* mode, of most epic and tragedy. [...]
> 4. If superior neither to other men nor to his environment, the hero is one of us: we demand from the poet the same canons of probability that we find in our own experience.[...]
> 5. If inferior in power or intelligence to ourselves, so that we have the sense of looking down on a scene of bondage, frustration of absurdity, the hero belongs to the *ironic* mode. (32-33)

Our focus is on the necessary link, since these are the phases of a cycle, between phase "5" and phase "1." Frye clarification that phase "1" occurs "as a rule" outside the realm of literature is not a concern since we are dealing with culture in the broadest sense. As we look for specific imagery related to our present cultural condition that we have assumed it is suspended between the end of a cycle and the beginning of the next, we find clusters of archetypes in the third essay of *Anatomy,* "Archetypal Criticism: Theory of Myths." The *pre-generic mythoi* or *archetypal narratives* corresponding to the *modes* of the historical cycle are the following, distinct in four categories: 1. Comedy; 2. Romance; 3 Tragedy; 4. Irony and satire. Each is associated to the seasons of the year (respectively: Spring, Summer, Fall, Winter), the periods of the day (morning, noon, evening, night), the periods of life (youth, maturity, old age, death).

At this point, if we define "ironic" the position of Bodei, linked to the Winter of modern philosophy, that has brought us the *pensiero debole* (feeble, weak thought, as expressed by Gianni Vattimo in the lucid darkness of his *transparent society*)[2], we begin to see how useful Fye's categories can be for us. They are, however, quite a few, and occasionally the terminology gets complicated. Adding extra flavours to an already overspiced stew, I am now presenting another set of categories of Frye's archetypal warehouse. Each of the four *mythoi* described above is divided in six different phases, but only the last of "4. Irony and satire" and the first of "1. Comedy" interest us.

> The sixth phase [of the "irony and satire" archetypal narrative] presents human life in terms of largely unrelieved bondage. Its setting features prisons, madhouse, lynching mobs, and places of execution, and it differs from a pure inferno mainly in the fact that in human experience suffering has an end in death. In our day the chief form of this phase is the nightmare of social tyranny, of which *1984* is perhaps the most familiar. We also find, on this boundary of the *visio malefica* the use of parody-religious symbols suggesting some form of Satan or Antichrist worship. In Kafka's *In the Penal Colony* a parody of original sin appears in the officer's remark, Guilt is never to be doubted." (*Anatomy of Criticism* 238)

This lead us to the following phase of the cycle, and that is the first phase of the "comedy" as archetypal narrative.

> We notice in ironic comedy that the demonic world is never far away. The rages of the *senex iratus* in Roman comedy are directed mainly at the tricky slave, who is threatened with the mill, with being flogged to death, with crucifixion, with having his head dipped in tar and set on fire, and the like, all penalties that could be and were exacted from slaves in life. An epilogue in Plautus inform us that the slave-actor who has blown up his lines will now be flogged; in one of Menander fragments a slave is tied up and burned with a torch on stage. One sometimes gets the impression that the audience of Plautus and Terence would have guffawed uproariously all through the Passion. We may ascribe this to the brutality of a slave society, but then we remember[...] *The Mikado*[...] *The Cocktail Party*[...] *The Lady's not for Burning*[...] Any reader can think of comedies in which the fear of death, sometimes a hideous death, hangs over the central character to the end, and is dispelled so quickly that one has almost the sense of awakening from nightmare. (*Anatomy of Criticism* 238)

---

[2] I am referring to *La società trasparente*, Vattimo's most popular book. For a detailed discussion, see my "Re-presenting Postmodernity: McLuhan for the Nineties," 173-76.

Of course Frye was more interested in showing the continuity of the cycle, rather than the opposition of two of its phases, but it is very clear that even with a smooth passage from one to the other there has to be a of reversal and a change in direction, as in the summersault and climbing of Dante at the bottom of Hell. Now that we have a good repertoire of symbols for the phase that precedes and for the one that follows the, we can concentrate our attention on the inertia at the centre of the process of transformation.

From End to Beginning: Anatomy of the Gap

The greatest reversal in the history of mankind must have been the coming of Christ. Again, we can get some inspiration from Northrop Frye:

> The time of Christ was [...] the period of the great consolidation of Classical literature under Virgil and Ovid. Here, as we should expect, the controlling imagery is that of the cyclical movement, which had expanded to take in such larger rhythms as the precession of the equinoxes. Hence there were many theories about a new cycle of history, just as there are theories about an "age of Aquarius" now. (*The Great Code* 96)

I don't know how serious Frye was with the comparison to contemporary theories of the "age of Aquarius," but it will be however useful to remember the connection, when we'll get to discuss the nature of Neobaroque or contemporary culture.

> The coming of Jesus into the world, then, seems to have taken place historically at one of those dialectical confrontations in which history suddenly expands to myth and indicates a dimension beyond the historical. (*Ibid.* 98)

Virgil and Ovid of course did not know Jesus, and the fact that they are witnesses and agents of the historical change brought by the beginning of Christianity leaves us with a phenomenon to observe for which we have no cause. We see, however, that Ovid's *Metamorphoses* represent the closing of a cycle that had begun with a mythological revelation. It all started, as in Vico's primordial times, with the personification of objects of nature: the sun, the moon, the earth, the sea, were identified with the divine bodies of Jupiter, Diana, Proserpina, Neptune *et cetera.* The transformations narrated in Ovid are reversed, and so you have the metamorphoses of Daphne into a laurel tree, of Adonis, Narcissus and Hyacinth into flowers. We have, then, at the end of the cycle, a retrieval of the primary process of transformation but with the reversed direction. We have also a great consolidation of knowledge, generally expressed in literature by works of the epic nature. And we have, finally, a crisis of history, which, as Frye puts it, "suddenly expands to myth" since it appears unable to contain or justify the extraordinary events of the present.

In terms of archetypes, Frye's *mythos* of Comedy tells us that the sexual imagery is central here, for it leads to marriage and progeny, and the transformation turns into to the establishment of a new society. In the case of the coming of Christ and the process of historical transformation beyond history of which it is at the centre, the union would be of Jesus with the Church as a bride:

> In the sixteenth century the conception of a transcending of the Church within history came into focus [...] The Church's role was to enter into a dialogue with the Word of God and not to replace it as the source of revelation. Milton, who, being a poet, understood the changes in metaphor were far more important than changes in doctrine, remarked that this involved thinking of the Church not as "mother" but as a young bride. (*Ibid.* 85-86)

Gap 1 = Baroque

We have all the elements we need to start looking at Baroque as the first of our two transformations. But first, we have to face this question, "why Baroque?" We know that there are cultural transformations and we know, or we assume that we know, that the pattern of all such transformations include a moment of inertia, or a gap, in which the line of "development" of culture reverses its direction... but we just have found no reason yet to be speaking of Baroque.

Perhaps, then, we should consider these two apparently opposite principles of the *Book of Ecclesiastes*. On the one hand we have that, "There is nothing new under the sun" (1.9); and on the other, "To every thing there is a season" (3.1). The first axioms points to the *process* of retrieval, and therefore to the recurring, cyclical nature of the transformational gaps, while the second points to the uniqueness of each transformation as independent *experience*, with its own particular identity. Baroque, therefore, is one of the many major transformations that have occurred in history, but it is unique in that it happened in a particular time and space. We can comfortably assume the setting is Italy and make the period (the broadest possible for the term "Baroque") span from 1550-1650.[3]

So we don't throw Eugenio D'Ors out of the window, nor do we discard Settembrini: for the first, Baroque is a "universal" category (opposed to classicism with which it alternates in the course of history), for the latter it is a unique historical aberration of human dignity, fostered by hypocrisy, fostered by the Jesuits; *Seicento* is therefore, for Settembrini, "Jesuitry of the arts."[4]

Which works of literature, art, music or architecture will we now choose to confirm our idea of Baroque? A good starting point could be painting, the real avant-garde of all the arts.[5] And it could be fascinating to see how, with the mannerists (by Wöllflin associated with the Baroque) the decadence becomes sublime and Renaissance becomes Baroque. Or perhaps we could start with Monteverdi to verify that by the humbling process of the *seconda pratica* (music at the service of poetry) music becomes superb. Or, perhaps, Baroque could easily be illustrated by confronting Bernini's and Borromini's ovals and spirals with Alberti's and Bramante's squares and circles, new churches with old temples. But these battles were all won, the questions settled, Baroque accepted and respected. The area of exploration and controversy is now literature, and in literature the king of Baroque, or "the king of the century" as Francesco De Sanctis called him, is the Neapolitan Cavalier Marino, author of *L'Adone*.

---

[3] Both "comfortable" assumptions are questionable. The time span is the widest possible and, as we shall see, there is a reason for that. As for the space, I chose to speak of Italy for practical reasons. I am not making José Antonio Maraval's nationalistic mistake, claiming that Baroque is uniquely Italian as he says that it is a Spanish thing (13-36), although my geographical limits would be more accurate than his, since you have no Baroque without Renaissance, and the Renaissance *is* a primarily Italian phenomenon.

[4] More details on these critics (and others) are in the still unsurpassed review of Baroque interpretarions by Giovanni Getto.

[5] I get this from Frye, "Wherever we turn in studying this art [painting], we are constantly brought up against the cave itself, as a shrouding maternal womb containing the embryos both of human society and of beings of the natural environment to which that society was most closely related. The persistence of the cave setting in Anatolia, India, Etruscan Italy, and many other places makes us wonder whether painting may not have a spacial relationship to the sense of something embryonic, present within the human civilization but suggesting the outlines of a human civilization not yet born." ("Literature and the Visual Arts," 194).

This poem was first conceived in the mind of the twenty-four year old Giovan Battista in 1593, three decades before becoming the *poema grande* that we know, and the longest poem—it has been said—of the entire Italian literature. The fundamental principle that informed the exuberant growth of the poem is a double faceted one. Conscious of the intellectual inheritance of the Renaissance, and fascinated by the new world of Galileo (whose *Saggiatore* appeared the same year of *L'Adone*, 1625), Marino chose to stay in the middle, indicating the new science with the old mythology, the future with the past. Ovid, his declared source of inspiration, supplied the dynamics of the change with the metamorphosis and, with it, the scattered structure of the epic and the narrative centrality of the sexual encounter between the Goddess of Love and the fifteen year old effeminate Adonis, whose delicate beauty attracts the wild boar, the true male of the poem (Pozzi 2.35), that kills him in an erotic embrace. Why such a story, such a myth, to symbolize an epochal cultural transformation? Giovanni Pozzi, introducing the critical edition of the poem, asks himself the same question:

> Gli anni [...] che si aprono sull'ultimo decennio del secolo [1500] e si chiudono con lo spirare del secondo che gli succede furono abitati da individualità sconvolgenti che rivoluzionarono i modi correnti della percezione e della sensibilità: Caravaggio, Galileo, Monteverdi, poco più indietro Tasso. Che ci sta a fare con tutto questo la fragile storia del giovinetto amato da Venere e ucciso da un porco? Che rappresenta fra quei bagliori l'esangue efebo tutto cascante di vezzi? E tuttavia la sua molle figura esercitò sui contemporanei un forte richiamo; poiché vi si avvicendarono, senza apparenti contatti, le massime menti poetiche di allora: Ronsard, Shakespeare, Lope de Vega. Lontanissimi l'uno dall'altro nello sviluppare la fama, conversero tutti nel sorprendervi uno stesso significato erotico e patetico:il fallimento dell'incontro sessuale come mezzo di umana intesa e uguaglianza, Ronsard avvilendo la donna, Shakespeare esaltando la riottosità del laspetti propri dell'uomo-eroe. [...] Qui siamo di fronte a convcergenze che hanno ler loro radici nel profondo della coscienza o dell'inconscio di un'epoca, a quell'allucinante processo per cui determinati motivi si fanno transitoriamente i portatori provolegiati dei sensi findamentali dell'esistenza. (7-8)

The thread of Ariadne that allows us not to get lost in the maze of Marino's imagery is the principle that Father Pozzi codified as *la legge del due* [the law of two] which I have used extensively and proved to sustain a wide spectrum of exegetical possibilities.[6]

Here are a few examples. The content of the poem is mythological but also historical for the insertion of actual events and character in the narration. The ancient referential values of the myth are kept but transformed with modern sensibility. The archetypal form is that of the tragedy, but in the end (in the last three cantos specifically) it turns into comedy. The philosophy, as Carlo Calcaterra first noticed (in his *Parnaso in rivolta* 90-93) is Platonic and Aristotelian at once. The literary genre is epic but the style is that of the lyric. The rhetorical figures are often presented in doubles, similies or metaphors with antitheses, alliterations with annominations, and therefore we are not surprised to find the chiasmus and the oximoron to testify the presence of unresolved ambiguities. Finally, the main characters themselves show a disconcerting ambiguity in their identity as well as in their role in the narration: Venus is defined by masculine attributes while Adonis is personified in the feminine.

Rather than solving the dichotomies, Marino accumulates them and intensifies the ambiguity of meaning. He defends his philosophical indetermination as the most prized quality of his poetry. His reluctance to offer unequivocal statements is programmatic. He says, at the beginning of the poem that poetry does not reveal the truth openly; rather, it hides it under "scorza mentita," false cover (*Adone* 1.10). It is therefore totally wrong to make him pay for his alleged lack of clarity. "Carebat philosophico ingenio" said of him the rational genius of Sforza Pallavicino (in his *Vindicationes*) and the negative judgment has accompanied the fortune, and misfortune of the poet for three centuries. We know better now. We know that Marino is situated in the interface of two different worlds and that, at least in the *milieu* of Italian literature, he is the most eloquent voice of the great transformation of his time.

I would love to indulge in some analytical work of Baroque imagery, but we have to move on swiftly and focus on the cause of the epochal metamorphosis precipitated and represented by *L'Adone*. Marshall McLuhan, drawing from Aquinas, taught us to distinguish between efficient and formal cause. The first gives the assurance of a precise passage

[6] "La legge del due si vede applicata ovunque nell'*Adone*; o, a meglio dire, si vedono ovunque delle coppie formate da elementi così disparati che, bisogna concluderne, se sono legati insieme con questo rapporto binario e non con uno diverso, devono esserlo per via di una costante stilistica che possiamo chiamare legge del due. (L'Adone 2.77). On the same topic see also Guardiani, "Inventio: Dal madrigale al poema grande" in *La meravigliosa retorica dell'*Adone.

between two events, between cause and effect in the common sense. But the mechanical coherence of this logic makes it, for our purpose, a deficient cause, if you allow me the pun. The concept is best employed to understand events of minimal scope and implies a margin of uncertainty which widens as new factors of the same phenomenon are discovered or simply discussed. To remain in the familiar realm of literary criticism, there is the risk to rely totally on a single "revealing" element (such as a particular rhetorical figure: think of "la metafora barocca" for instance which, incidentally, is a title of a book that I found completely useless), the risk of oversimplifying with a stylistic trait a broad phenomenon that refuses to be contained in such a tight cast. The concept of formal cause, on the other hand, is at best with broad phenomena which can be defined from a *dossier* of contemporary events, fragmented as they may appear at first, from which it is possible to extract a common denominator, or the formal cause, since the event, in the study of culture, always comes before the consciousness of the cause.

Now, for McLuhan the greatest cultural transformation occurred in our millennium, prior to the advent of electric media, was determined by the printing press, which is then the most important, encompassing and lasting formal cause of the cultural events following its inception in the second half of the fifteenth century. But the knowledge of the cause, we just said, always comes after the event has taken place, and the more powerful, profound and wide reaching the medium, the slower its recognition will be. The new medium is very much present however, but operates only in a subliminal fashion until its identity will finally emerge in the collective consciousness. Only then, or from then, it will be applied with a reliable cognition of its effects. A couple of example will clarify this rather abstract but fundamental point.

In the first years of typography it was not uncommon to hand copy published books in order to give them the "dignity" of a "real book," that is of a manuscript. This indicates a vision of reality projected backwards which McLuhan defines as "the rear-view mirror syndrome." We see it in action again when the first automobile started to roam the road. It was called "horseless carriage" evoking the world of haystacks and dirt roads rather than the new world of highways, motels and suburban settlements.

We need more than a century, to go back to our argument, to reach that phase of development that McLuhan calls of "applied technology," which brings us to the years of Marino, Shakespeare and Bacon, Lope and Góngora (all born in the same decade, 1560s and most active around the end of the century). Incidentally, it is most interesting that Amedeo Quondam, in his exhaustive, "La letteratura in tipografia" opens the essay with Francis Bacon's *Novum Organum* (1620) to indicate a mature consciousness of the effects of the (not so new anymore) typographic medium.

A detailed inventory of these effects is in McLuhan's *Gutenberg Galaxy*. Suffice it here to recall the following: first of all, a democratization of culture with a new emphasis on the individual perception; moreover, an anatomical fragmentation of the objects in the perception of reality, corresponding to an equally revolutionary fragmentation of the aesthetic experience; and finally, a new technicism in the arts and the use the language leading to great debates on literary genres and to the production of the first Italian dictionary.

Now the moment of applied technology, in which we have placed Marino and his contemporary is not a single point in time in which we spot a conscious change of direction, but rather a quite ample season of overlapping, albeit contrasting, tendencies. And this is exactly where we have to focus to capture the essence of the transformation. We are at the interface of the late Renaissance and the early enlightenment, a moment of uncertainties and ambiguities that favored blitz and metamorphoses in all aspects of cultural life. As the two cultures of manuscript and typography come to a final confrontation we witness, in McLuhan's words, "the crossing, or hybridization of media with the release of a great new force as by fission of fusion"(cf. *Understanding media*, chapter 5, "Hybrid Energy"). We shall recall this vortex of energy, in Marino best exemplified by the stubborn tension-building unresolved dichotomy of the "law of two," as we turn to the parallel revolution of the electric media that we define as Neobaroque.

Gap 2 Neobaroque

In ideal agreement with Pozzi's law of two, we find here, to caption the rest of the picture, the praise of the double by Windham Lewis [from *Blast N. 1*, 1914]:

> You must talk with two tongues, if you do not wish to cause confusion.
> There is nothing so impressive as the number TWO.
> You must be a duet in everything.
> For the Individual, the single object, and isolated, is, you must admit, an absurdity.
> Why try and give the impression of a consistent and indivisible personality?

The double personality indicated by Lewis is a critical reality destined to enlighten every aspect of the cultural life of the twentieth century. McLuhan refers to it to illustrate the contemporary creative and dynamic relation that the *double* establishes between the *cliché* and the *archetype*, or, with the terms of gestalt psychology, between *figure* and *ground* (text and context, medium and message).

More than a century after Gutenberg, as already mentioned, we had to wait for the new medium of typography to flex its muscle and come to the epochal confrontation with the previous medium that led to the Baroque metamorphosis. And more than a century, again, we had to wait for the electric technology to bring us here, in the middle of another no doubt greater metamorphosis. The very same technology that brought the telegraph gave us the computer, after a fast paced march through telephone, radio, and television. And it is only now, now that the electromagnetic medium, with the computer, has touched the lives of billions of people that we are caught in the middle of another cultural confrontation. The old medium is now print, stubbornly resisting the bytes of history (pun intended). So, again, we are in the eye of the storm. And the vortex of energy that the oppositional forces generate is again the theater of blitz and metamorphoses.

I can't even begin to describe the effects of the ongoing transformation. But you only have to look around you to find them. The old *querelle des anciennes et des modernes* has returned with disquieting implications. The idea of progress as lineal development has vanished, and so is the chronological sequence structure of history. Of all the people who have dealt with this cultural condition, two have specifically referred to it as Neobaroque, Omar Calabrese (cf. *L'età neobarocca*) and Severo Sarduy ("El barroco y el neobarroco,") both lacking, in my opinion, a solid theoretical framework for their fundamentally correct analyses. It is interesting to verify in them a real obsession with the representation of the body, the human body that fascinated Marino in *L'Adone*. In the seventeenth century poem, with the hybridism of the main characters, we even find a physical anatomy of the human organism. The modern critics, on their part, insist on the relationship between the shape of the body and the psychology associated with it, from body building, in Calabrese, to gender crossing, in Sarduy (especially in his latest works of fiction). McLuhan, in this regard, spoke of *discarnation*, resulting from the instantaneous projection that the electric media make of the human body diffusing the icon in the world of telecommunication, in the global village, now Internet, the widest place "immarginable."

To recap

Baroque leads to modernity while Neobaroque moves away from it. Is this an invalidation of the similarities we have indicated? On the contrary, the dynamics of the change characterize both phenomena as interfaces, and as center of innovative forces, regardless of the different direction the rush of creativity will take.

The formal cause that for Baroque transformation was the printing press is now, for Neobaroque, the electric medium. From Kafka to Joyce, from Cézanne to De Chirico we have had countless of intuitive demonstrations of the epochal transformation in which we are now immersed. At the present time, in the phase of applied technology, we have verified their prophecies and live in a stage of unsettling, and perhaps even frightening instability. The new Cassandras (Alvin Toffler for one) predict decades, if not centuries of gloom: the classless society, the democratic society that we have come to accept as the logical and irreversible development of human society is in danger. The very same institutions of which most of us here are part, as print users and producers, are decaying if not in spirit, in economic health. We are, and it is clear to everyone, on the verge of a massive epochal change. So, again, we are in a hybrid situation, not unlike that of the late 1500s in the entire European context. We have more consciousness of where we are going but our vision of the future is still blurred until, at least, we make good use of the process we have learned and train our sensibility to face the effects of the metamorphosis. History, after all, tells us that we have been here before.

WORKS CITED

Bodei, Remo. *Se la storia ha un senso*. Bergamo: Moretti e Vitali, 1997.

Calabrese, Omar. *L'età neobarocca*. Bari: Laterza, 1987.

Calcaterra, Carlo. *Il Parnaso in rivolta*. Milano: Mondadori, 1940.

Frye, Northrop. "Literature and the Visual Arts," in *Myth and Metaphor: Selected Essays 1974-1988*. Ed. Robert D. Denham. Charlottesville and London: UPof Virginia, 1990. 183-95.

__________. *Anatomy of Criticism: Four Essays*. Princeton: Princeton UP, 1957.

__________. *The Great Code: The Bible and Literature*. Toronto: Academic Press, 1992.

Getto, Giovanni. "La polemica sul Barocco," in *Letteratura italiana. Le correnti*. Milano: Marzorati, 1975. 417-504.

Guardiani, Francesco. "Re-presenting Postmodernity: McLuhan for the Nineties," in *Mediating Culture: The Politics of Representation*. William Anselmi and Kosta Gouliamos eds. Toronto–Montréal–New-York, 1994. 151-84.

_________. *La meravigliosa retorica dell'"Adone" di G.B. Marino*. Firenze: Olschki, 1989.

Maravall, José Antonio. "Introduzione. La cultura del Barocco come concetto di epoca," in *La cultura del Barocco*. Bologna: Mulino, 1985.

Marino, Giovan Battista. *L'Adone*. Ed. Giovanni Pozzi. 2 voll. Milano: Mondadori, 1976.

McLuhan, Marshall. *The Gutenberg Galaxy: The Making of Typographic Man*. Toronto: U of Toronto P, 1962.

_________. *Understanding Media*. New York: McGraw-Hill, 1964.

Pozzi, Giovanni. See Marino, Giovan Battista.

Quondam, Amedeo. "La letteratura in tipografia," *Letteratura italiana*. Ed. Alberto Asor Rosa. Vol. II. Torino: Einaudi, 1983: 555-686.

Sarduy, Severo. "El barroco y el neobarroco," *America Latina en su Literatura*. Buenos Aires: Siglo XXI, 1974, 167-84.

Vattimo, Gianni. *La società trasparente*. Milano: Garzanti, 1989.

John H. Simpson

A Scrapbook of Lessons for the Modern from the (New) Baroque: Discontinuity, Gazing, Glancing, Listening

ABSTRACT. From Descartes to Weber, modernity has foregrounded (and celebrated) the rational subject and the notion of rational action apart from any theological horizon. Christine Buci-Gluckmann's interpretation of the work of Walter Benjamin and, especially, the 'meditations' on Paul Klee's *Angelus Novus*, is an argument of reading modernity as a field of angelic presence uncanniness, allegory, pastiche, parody, irony and ambivalence—in other words, as a field of Baroque Reason that implies the hidden Other. This presentation explores Buci-Gluckmann's argument and its connection with the theme of religious hope.

What can the Baroque teach the Modern? That the Modern is no longer fashionable because it has been replaced by the New Baroque? Indeed, line *has* become curve, pastiche *is* in vogue, and we *do* learn from Las Vegas (Venturi and Scott-Brown, 1972).

The *barroco*, the imperfect pearl, once again attracts the glances of Western civilization. The best building of our time according to the dean of American architects, Philip Johnson, is Frank Gehry's Guggenheim Museum Bilbao (*Figures 1 & 2*). It billows and sways "like a Modernist rectilinear structure seen in a fun-house mirror" (Dault, 1998:C18). Bilbao—the perfect imperfect pearl—leaves no doubt that we live in an age when the Modern is being re-formed or de-formed depending on your point of view (cf. Jameson, 1991:55-66).

Bilbao seems to be an allegory for all sorts of contemporary things. Freese (1998) points out the difficulty that social theorists have in overcoming Cartesian dualism and constructing humans as complex beings between nature and culture. The Cartesian 'temptation' that underwrites the modern presupposition that we can be analyzed and explained as either reasoning psycho-social machines or metaboliz-

Going for Baroque: Cultural Transformations1550-1650.
A St. Michael's College Symposium. Francesco Guardiani ed. Ottawa: Legas, 1999

ing/reproducing machines still retains its grip. While giving lip service to the un-Cartesian presupposition that humans ought to be theorized as the complex in-betweeness of nature and culture, some theorists "still cling like Linus to his blanket ... to positing mechanistic explanations" (318) that can't possibly account for what we are as humans *else such explanations would have done so already.*

Freese's recognition of the (unstable) conjunction of the presupposition of human in-betweeness as a starting point for social theory and the continuing addiction in theoretical practice to the modern "Linus blanket" of Cartesian mechanistic linearity resembles the swaying deformed lines of Bilbao. Linearity is still there but it is linearity that has been deprived of its rectilinear dominance and adequacy as it circles and droops on the way to an unknown future.

Constructed from *within* modernity and periodized from, say, 1550 to 1700, the first Baroque can be viewed as a cultural halfway house, a refuge by the side of the road on the way from the Renaissance to the intimations of modernity in the classic revival and the romantic movement. In this view the Baroque is located within the scope of modernity's ontic regime of time where a sense of continuity arises (paradoxically) from radical discontinuity. Moderns recognize the past—indeed, they are the constructors of the past they recognize—but in modernity the past is merely a negative resource for the construction of the future. The past is not perfected. The past is not an honourable but incomplete present, a presence to be re-molded and shaped according to a telos of perfection. The past does not collaborate in the construction of the future.

In the ontic regime of modern time the past is a presence to be overcome, defeated and destroyed on the way to the future. "Italy has been for too long the great market of the secondhand dealer. We want to rid it of the unnumerable museums that cover it with innumerable cemeteries" (Marinneti, 1988 [1909]:99). This is called Progress. Modernity demands the new and modernity sees the new in the progression from Renaissance to Mannerism to Baroque to Rococco (cf. Sypher, 1955).

> Modernity's urge for discontinuity achieved by the lethal imposition of homogeneity (the creation of the same through destruction of the different) in the name of deformed justice or satanic purity (Marx, 1954 [1848]; Hitler, 1943 [1925]) matured in the horrible, evil ripeness of the Shoah with its destruction of the chosen others who are 'not ours' (Simpson, 1996:3; 1997; cf. Adorno and Horkheimer, 1972:168-208).

Forever seized by the memory of radical discontinuity and, hence, caught on the cusp of modernity in its most extreme form *and* at the same time existing in the daily memory and reconstruction of tradition and its praxis, the Jews are the living bearers *par excellence* of the New Baroque as a mode of action: the pastiche of the remembered modern radical discontinuity of liquidation and the daily presence of the practice of tradition that is *both* a rightful mockery and a redeeming condemnation of the dark heart of modernity *and* an orientation in freedom to the horizon of the future (as long as the Messiah tarries).

While migration is not liquidation, it is a form of radical social and existential discontinuity. The New Baroque sensibility of jumbled mixtures and hodgepodge—a sensibility that is the lived reality of migration—underwrites the aesthetic of Salman Rushdie's (1988) *The Satanic Verses*, an aesthetic, it should be observed, that has provoked the *modern* homogenizing response of the *fatwah*.

II

Modernity is an ontic regime of time. It is also an ontic regime of space. However, where the unity of modern time is derived from discontinuity, modern space is the unity of the smooth continuous linear path traversed by the eye as it moves from foreground to vanishing point. This, of course, is the familiar ocular field of the Renaissance, a scopic regime that according to Martin Jay (1992) is also the hegemonic visual and, hence, spatial model of the modern era as well. In modernity space is rectilinear. Its abstractions are drawn together (paradoxically) by the uniformity of an 'underlying' surface, e.g. *Figure 3*. Modern space is conceived in the manner of a lone eye looking through a peephole at the scene in front of it. It follows the logic of the steady Gaze rather than the moving Glance, thus producing a visual take that is eternalized, disembodied and reduced to one point of view.

The monocular Gaze of the Renaissance and its continuation as an hegemonic scopic regime in modernity embraces universality and a transcendental perspective. It is consistent with Cartesian ideas of subjective rationality. It is not without its detractors. Thus, Nietzsche gleefully concluded that if everyone had his or her own camera obscura, each with a distinctly different peephole, then no transcendental worldview was possible (Jay, 1992:184; cf., Lyotard, 1984).

Martin Jay (1992) argues a somewhat different case. The hegemony of the ocular Renaissance model continues in modernity, but other models of space and vision persist as well. Following the contemporary French philosopher, Christine Buci-Glucksmann (1984), Jay identifies the most radical of the persistent models of space and vision with the Baroque which he contrasts with the Renaissance model of unity, harmony and perspective.

> In opposition to the lucid, linear, solid, fixed, planimetric, closed form of the Renaissance... the baroque was painterly, recessional, soft-focused, multiple and open. Derived, at least according to one standard etymology, from the Portuguese word for an irregular, oddly shaped pearl, the baroque connoted the bizarre and peculiar, traits which were normally disdained by the champions of clarity and transparency of form .... Baroque vision sought to represent the unrepresentable and necessarily failing produced *the melancholy that Walter Benjamin in particular saw as characteristic of baroque sensibility*. As such, it was closer to what a long tradition of aesthetics called the sublime, in contrast to the beautiful, because of its yearning for a presence that can never be fulfilled (187-88; emphasis added).

A close reading of Benjamin associates melancholy not only with the aesthetic tradition of the sublime, that is with the substitution of the absence of presence for God, but also with the 'vacuum' created where the link between the transcendent meaning of good works and civic action is severed. Walter Benjamin (1892-1940) was the first twentieth century intellectual to analyze the Baroque and appropriate its aesthetic as, in effect, a form of social analysis and critique. *The Origin of German Tragic Drama* (*Ursprung des deutschen Trauerspeils*) was published in Berlin in 1928 (English translation 1977). It is a study of the mourning plays (*Trauerspiels*) written in the middle of the seventeenth century by playwrights mainly of the Silesian school.

The playwrights of the *Trauerspiels* were Lutheran. They wrote in response to the Counter-Reformation, the Thirty Year's War and the rise of the nation-state that followed the Peace of Westphalia. The

Baroque of the *Trauerspiels*, however, was not the 'sunny' Baroque where the absolute prince and the Counter-Reformation held sway. Rather it was the Baroque that was in thrall to the bleak rule of a melancholic distaste for life.

Beniamin writes:

> Whereas in the decades of the Counter-Reformation Catholicism had penetrated secular life with all the power of its discipline, the relationship of Lutheranism to the everyday has always been antinomic. The rigorous morality of its teaching in respect of civic conduct stood in sharp contrast to its renunciation of 'good works.' By denying the latter any special miraculous spiritual effect, making the soul dependent on grace through faith and making the secular-political sphere a testing ground for a life which was only indirectly religious, being intended for the demonstration of civic virtues, it did, it is true, instil into the people a strict sense of obedience to duty, but in its great men it produced melancholy. Even in Luther himself, the last two decades of whose life are filled with an increasing heaviness of soul, there are signs of a reaction against the assault on good works. 'Faith,' of course, carried him through, but it did not prevent life from becoming stale. 'What is a man, | If his chief good and market of his time | Be but to sleep and feed? a beast, no more. | Sure, he that hath made us with such large discourse, | Looking before and after, gave us not | That capability and god-like reason | To fust in us unused.' These words of Hamlet contain both the philosophy of Wittenberg and a protest against it. In that excessive reaction which ultimately denied good works as such, and not just their meritorious and penitential character, there was an element of German paganism and the grim belief in the subjection of man to fate. Human actions were deprived of all value. Something new arose: an empty world (1977:138-9).

Benjamin's association of melancholy with the ultimate meaninglessness of civic acts in the secularized "naked public square" (Neuhaus, 1984) has a decided postmodern ring to it. If hysteria was the reigning malady of triumphant nineteenth century modernity, surely melancholy is the popular disease of Baroque postmodernity. We call it depression (Kramer, 1993). Benjamin enables us to see the tie between Bilbao and Prozac and to understand the malaise that arises from the broken link between our civic, public actions and God's boundaries in

His-Her time, *Jetztzeit*, the time of the eternal now (Benjamin, 1968; Tillich, 1963).

III

Benjamin purchased Paul Klee's watercolour, "Angelus Novus," (*Figure 4*) in Munich in 1920. It is clear from his writings and the writings of others who knew him—in particular Gershom Scholem—that "Angelus Novus" presented an image to Benjamin that seized him throughout his life. In his writings Benjamin put up at least two interpretations of "Angelus Novus"—I will deal with only one here—that were anchored, ultimately, in the angelology of the kabbalah, the body of mystical Jewish writings where it is related

> that in every instant God creates an immense number of new angels whose only purpose is, before they dissolve into naught, to sing His praise before His throne for a moment. Mine [his angel—JHS], Benjamin says, was interrupted in doing so (Scholem, 1976:205).

Near the end of his life (taken by his own hand in 1940 as he fled the Nazis advancing in France only to be stopped at the Spanish border), Benjamin wrote:

> A Klee painting named "Angelus Novus" shows an angel looking as though he is about to move away from something he is fixedly contemplating. His eyes are staring, his mouth is open, his wings are spread. This is how one pictures the angel of history. His face is turned toward the past. Where we perceive a chain of events, he sees one single catastrophe which keeps piling wreckage upon wreckage and hurls it in front of his feet. The angel would like to stay, awaken the dead and make whole what has been smashed. But a storm is blowing from Paradise; it has got caught in his wings with such violence that the angel can no longer close them. This storm irresistibly propels him into the future to which his back is turned, while the pile of debris before him grows skyward. This storm is what we call progress (Benjamin, 1968:259-60).

Benjamin sees the Modern ontic regime of time in "Angelus Novus": the destruction of the present on the way to the future. Does the New Baroque also appear? Of course, one could argue that any appropriation of an angel leads back to Baroque sensibility where angels hold serious sway. I want to make a different case.

Compare the features of "Novus Angelus" with the features of another Klee painting, "Head of a Man" (*Figure 5*). The eyes in "Head of a Man" display the Renaissance/Modern Gaze, the look of visual dominance in the service of subjective rationality reducing everything to its own point of view. (Some would call that "fundamentalism" (cf. Simpson, 1992; 1994)).

There is a lot of eye in "Head of a Man." There are no ears. Subjective rationality does not listen. It only Gazes and appropriates. "Angelus Novus," on the other hand, is not a Gazing angel. It Glances ever so slightly. One eye looks at the wreckage of the past lying before it. The other eye drifts to something at the side of history. There is a Baroque multiplicity of visual realities in "Angelus Novus" *and unlike "Head of a Man" the New Angel has ears*. S/he can see *and* hear. We see a Glancing and Listening angel in "Angelus Novus." What is the meaning of this?

"Angelus Novus" can, ultimately, be framed in the creation narrative, itself, *where God speaks before seeing*. "And God said, Let there be light: and there was light. And God saw the light, that it was good...." Word is the source of light in the time of the eternal now. According to the Christian appropriation, "In the beginning was the Word.... in him was life, and the life was the light of men."

Benjamin's angel is a Glancing angel. It is also a Listening angel, Listening to the Word in the rush of history. To moderns that may seem bizarre and peculiar—a bit Baroque—in an age when the image (the graven image?) still rules (Simpson, 1998), but rules—as Bilbao tells us—in the shade of the twilight of Modernity.

Moderns only Gaze. They do not Listen. In its Baroque multiplicity Benjamin's "Angelus Novus" tells them that it is possible to listen (to the Word), too.

WORKS CITED

Benjamin, Walter. *The Origin of German Tragic Drama*. London: New Left Books, 1977 [1928].

__________, *Illuminations*. New York: Harcourt, Brace & World, 1968.

Buci-Glucksmann, Christine. *Baroque Reason: The Aesthetics of Modernity*. London: SAGE Publications, 1994.

Dault, Gary Michael. "Designing On A Large Scale." *The Globe and Mail*. Toronto, Ontario. February 21 C18, 1998.

Freese, Lee. Review of *Human By Nature: Between Biology and the Social Sciences*. Eds. Peter Weingart, Sandra D. Mitchell, Peter J. Richerson, and Sabine Maasen. Mahwah, NJ: Lawrence Erlbaum, 1997. *Contemporary Sociology* 27.3(1998): 317-18.

Hitler, Adolf. *Mein Kampf*. Boston MA: Houghton Mifflin, 1943 [1925].

Horkheimer, Max and Theodor W. Adorno. *Dialectic of Enlightenment*. New York: Continuum, 1988 [1944].

Jameson, Frederic. *Postmodernism, or, The Cultural Logic of Late Capitalism*. Durham, NC: Duke UP, 1991.

Jay, Martin. "Scopic Regimes of Modernity." *Modernity and Identity*. Eds. Scott Lash and Jonathan Friedman. Oxford UK & Cambridge USA: Blackwell, 1992. 178-195

Kramer, Peter D. *Listening to Prozac*. New York: Viking Penguin, 1993.

Lyotard, Jean-François. *The Postmodern Condition: A Report on Knowledge*. Manchester: Manchester UP, 1984.

Marinneti, Filippo Tommaso. "Futurist Manifesto" (excerpt). *Art of Our Century*. Ed. Jean-Louis Ferrier. New York: Prentice Hall Press. 1988 [1909], 99.

Marx, Karl. *The Communist Manifesto*. Chicago: Henry Regerny Company, 1954 [1848].

Neuhaus, Richard John. *The Naked Public Square: Religion and Democracy in America*. Grand Rapids, MI: W.B. Eerdmans Publishing Co, 1984.

Rushdie, Salman. *The Satanic Verses*. New York: Viking Penguin, 1988.

Scholem, Gershom. *On Jews and Judaism in Crisis: Selected Essays*. New York: Schocken Books, 1976.

Simpson, John H. "Fundamentalism Re-visited: The Fading of Modernity as a Source of Symbolic Capital." *Religion and Politics in Comparative Perspective: Revival of Religious Fundamentalism in East and West*. Eds. Bronislaw Misztal and Anson Shupe. New York: Praeger, 1992. 3-27.

__________. Review of *Fundamentalisms and the State: Remaking Politics, Economics, and Militance*. Eds. Martin E. Marty and R. Scott Appleby.

Chicago: U of Chicago P. *Journal for the Scientific Study of Religion* 33(1994): 338-89.

__________. "Introduction: Difference, the State, and Society in Contemporary Canada." *Multiculturalism, Jews and Identities in Canada.* Eds. Howard Adelman and John H. Simpson . Jerusalem: Magnes Press. 1996. 1-10.

__________. "The Social Construction of Plagues." *CONCILIUM: An international review of theology* 273(1997): 17-29.

__________. "Confessions, Outings, and Ordeals: Understanding Media in the United States." *Religion, Mobilization, and Social Actions.* Eds. Anson Shupe and Bronislaw Misztal. Westport, CT: Praeger, 1988. 216-227.

Sypher, Wylie. *Four Stages of Renaissance Style: Transformation in Art and Literature 1400-1700.* Garden City, NY: Doubleday, 1995.

Tillich, Paul. *The Eternal Now.* New York: Scribner, 1963.

Venturi, Robert and Denise Scott-Brown. *Learning From Las Vegas.* Cambridge, MA: MIT Press, 1972.

FIGURE 1. GUGGENHEIM MUSEUM BILBAO, FRANK GEHRY

FIGURE 2. GUGGENHEIM MUSEUM BILBAO, FRANK GEHRY

FIGURE 3. *ABSTRACT WATERCOLOR*, WASSILI KANDINSKY

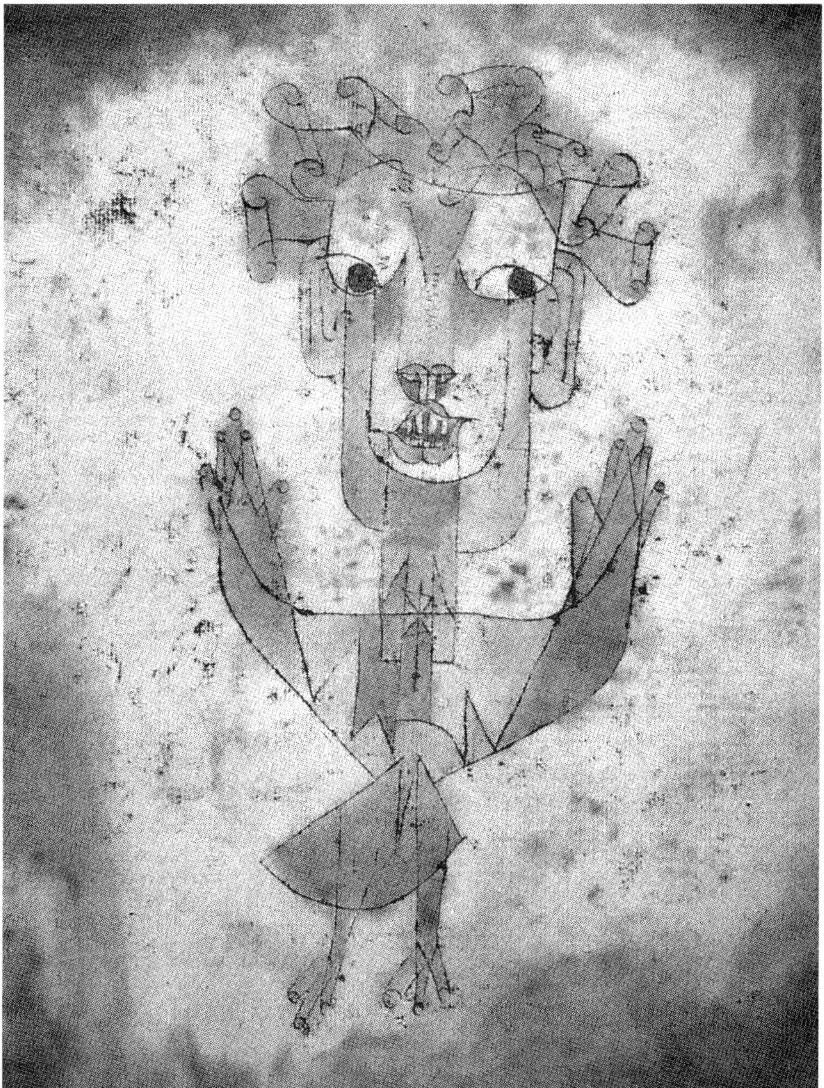

FIGURE 4. *ANGELUS NOVUS*, PAUL KLEE

FIGURE 5. *HEAD OF A MAN*, PAUL KLEE

Donald J. Lococo

Baroque Science: The Lens on Infinity

ABSTRACT. Advances in science and technology emerged into the consciousness of Baroque Europe through the adaptation of lens technology for use in scientific discovery. The perfection of the telescope and microscope made possible accurate optical measurements and the discovery of a vastly more wondrous universe than that of the Medieval cosmos. These discoveries were not only scientific in the modern sense but inspired a differentiation of human consciousness. The knowledge of the micro–universe revealed by the microscope and the vastness of the cosmos, as observed by the telescope, indelibly changed human consciousness. Revelation of God in the Christian method is deepened by an ever greater knowledge of the created order. Through increased understanding of God's work, Christian Culture ever grows in knowledge to better understand faith in the Divinity of Jesus Christ.

Throughout the Baroque period, advances in science and technology emerged into the collective consciousness of Europe through the adaptation of lens technology for use in scientific discovery. The perfection of the telescope and microscope made accurate optical measurements possible and led to the discovery of a vastly more wondrous universe than that of the Medieval cosmos. These discoveries inspired a differentiation of human consciousness. What was once considered finite and known became nearly infinite and unknown.

I believe that optics may well have been the single factor that shifted scientific inquiry towards a primarily empirical methodology. As a result, human creativity generated an optics–altered diversify and greatly expanded the collective imagination. In optical imagery, those who attempted to characterize the Transcendental had a new technology to exploit in literary and theological discussion. During the Baroque, the emergence of sophisticated optical instruments gave early modern scientists an increased understanding of the universe.

Going for Baroque: Cultural Transformàtions1550-1650.
A St. Michael's College Symposium. Francesco Guardiani ed. Ottawa: Legas, 1999

This greatly aided Christian Culture to better understand faith in the Divinity of Jesus Christ, where the mystery of God and creation unite.

Our modern understanding of science and technology is the product of a muddle of information from a variety of sources: some of it reliable, some of it not. This is one of the problems of the so–called information age. Our easy access to the Internet in no way guarantees that the information retrieved is reliable. And the media exploit the reporting of science and technology for its "gee wiz" effect, often merging the contributions of both into a misleading mediocrity. Popular awareness of science and technology is so far removed from the primary sources that report the actual research that we lose sight of the fact that science and technology are very distinct phenomena. Each is the product of human imagination and empirical methods. However, each represents the end point of different human traditions which extend back to prehistory.

Stephen F. Mason, in his book "The History of the Sciences" (1962) draws a distinction between the craft tradition and the scholarly tradition of human accomplishment. The craft tradition has its source in the tool–making abilities of human invention and socio–biology. According to Mason, the scholarly tradition began with the ancient Greeks, who asked the first philosophical questions in Western civilization and recorded them in their writings. Clearly, the craft tradition had its beginnings thousands of years earlier; and was perhaps even pre–human in its origins.

In short, technology is the modern end–product of the craft tradition, but modern science is a product of both craft and scholarly traditions combined. The development of the scientific method out of the scholarly tradition's emphasis on the primacy of the text required the recognition of empiricism as a vital part of a distinctly scientific scholarship. This was a pastime not fully acceptable to natural philosophers from the late Middle Ages well into the Renaissance. In fact, during the Baroque period, the stand–off between the so–called Aristotelians and the early scientists, such as Galileo and Kepler, marked the emergence of modern science from the marriage of these two traditions. The role of the church in the resistance to Galileo's findings was more symptomatic of the battle between the two approaches rather than causative.

One might argue that technological discovery is distinct from that of scientific discovery. However, that would be too simplistic a conclusion, because sometimes our greatest technologists were also our greatest scientists, especially so during the Baroque period.

Galileo Galilei was an example of scientist who first succeeded as a technologist. Before his perfection of the telescope, how much experience Galileo had with theoretical optics and practical experience with lenses have been difficult to ascertain. Certainly, the craft of lens–making pre–dates Galileo's perfection of the telescope by at least three–centuries.

We don't know who invented lenses per se and precisely when the discovery was made. By the year 1290, the invention of spectacles came to the aid of those who until then lived much of their lives with blurred vision. Some Italian historians claim that the inventor of spectacles was Salvino D'Armato of Florence. He was a craftsman and these artisans rarely published the results of their discoveries. There was no documentary proof that spectacles were invented by D'Armato, except for an inscription on his tombstone (Ford 1985).

Spectacles may have been the first practical invention of the Middle Ages to have its first use in a non–military setting. However there developed a diversity of uses for lenses. This re–introduction of lens technology was a turning point in the history of empirical inquiry which later would give rise to new sciences.

It was roughly three hundred years after the introduction of spectacles before the telescope was invented by someone in Holland, again we do not know whom. It was not until Galileo appropriated this design, laboured in a workshop for supposedly twenty–four hours to perfect it, that a workable telescope was produced which had scientific applicability. What was more, his first use of the instrument was to impress a politician of its military applications. This was the means by which he gained the Baroque equivalent of tenure at the University of Padua. How things have changed.

Not until he was well established in professional and financial security did Galileo even address a scientific hypothesis using his invention. Then he turned his telescope towards the heavens and immediately made enormous contributions to the ancient science of astronomy. Until Galileo built his telescope, the advancement of astronomy had reached a standstill because of the limitations of the unaided human eye. In the generation before Galileo, Tycho Brahe had made over a thousand measurements of stars in his life. Yet, despite his accuracy, there was still over 1% error in his measurements made without visual magnification (Boorstin 1985). Kepler gathered very little data of his own before Galileo sent him a telescope as a gift. The telescope's entry into the astronomers' bag of tricks significantly increased the accuracy of measurement. Yet this was not what brought about the revolution in astronomy

That night when Galileo trained his telescope on Jupiter and over the course of several nights of observation noticed four satellites orbiting the planet, he realized that this was utterly new. Few were neutral about his discoveries. The so–called Aristotelians criticized him because his observations might lead to conclusions which could contradict the Ptolmaic theory of the universe. It had been a generally accepted norm of Christian piety that you must not believe evidence of your eyes over the truths of revelation.

Vasco Ronchi, a modern Galileo scholar, has claimed that the sense of touch was the final avenue of empirical verification prior to the scientific revolution. Medieval philosophers distrusted the sense of vision as a means of confirming evidence (Ronchi 1967). It was not surprising that at first, optical instruments were not recognized as valid either. Some believed that they produced evidence that was tantamount to a magnified lie. This claim was not entirely groundedless. Telescope lenses in use prior to Galileo's vast improvements in design and lens quality produced a magnified blur. In this vein, one fairly valid criticism of Galileo's observed "moons" was that they might be a product of the distortion effect of the lens.

It is true that no lens was a perfect magnifier of the object observed, even today. The lenses of Galileo's time were hand–made and had no correction for inherent imperfections that we now know lenses have because of the imperfect nature of the materials of which they are made. So it was true that a telescopic image was not precisely true to the object viewed. However, that meant that the object viewed was only imprecise, not a phantom of the eyes. No true lens can create an image that is not there.

Galileo's discovery of the moons of Jupiter was a true turning point in inquiry. The problem with his generation as opposed to that of Copernicus was the intervening Reformation which made Rome very leery of the appearance of any undefined dogma. Despite all scholarly and unscholarly attempts to divert this turning point in our understanding of the universe, eventually the Copernican revolution reached its resolution in the 19th century, when the Copernican theory was demonstrated quite conclusively with the measurement of stellar parallax (Boorstin 1985). This opened up to the world the universe of the nearly infinitely distant and infinitely large.

It is clear that technological advance is a different phenomenon of discovery than that of the scientific. Technology can lead to new science when it gives rise to new ways to viewing the universe. The lens did this figuratively and literally. Certainly the lens show human beings aspects of creation which have always been there but have been invisible to our ancestors prior to Galileo's discoveries. Lenses do not show us new things but timeless things of which we are ignorant and which Christian revelation has not directly disclosed.

This realization was a breakthrough in human imagination. In the case of the telescope, the report of satellites orbiting Jupiter revolutionized our understanding of the universe. Quite simply, the ancients had been wrong. Truth had to be confirmed by observation despite what the ancients said about the issue. The telescope had provided human beings with a view of cosmic things at great distances and times which were distinct from our own. It gave us a view of eternity which humanity had thought up until then was only a God's–eye view.

Similar breakthroughs occurred with the use of lenses applied to the microscopic universe. Within a generation of Galielo, Antony Leeuwenhoek, a simple draper in Holland, built and used simple one–lens microscopes which revolutionized our understanding of life and matter. He was the first to report the existence of microorganisms, both single–celled and multi–celled. He was the first to describe the cellular structure of plants and animals; the first to describe sperm and eggs; the first to describe the fine features of insects, textiles and hair and feathers (Ford 1985). He unfolded a whole world of concrete reality which no one even suspected existed.

From Leeuwenhoek and Galileo and his successors, intellectual excitement ignited by visual wonders became the impetus of scientists that drove them on to new discovery. However, like the telescope, it took nearly a century for the microscope to be taken seriously by the public as well as a greater cross–section of the scientific community. Certainly the immense effect upon the scientific world and the great expansion of our understanding of the micro–cosmos spilled into the world of literature. Newton's optics became applied as a metaphor in widespread use in English poetry written during his time. Visual imagery from the micro–perspective emerged in Baroque Italian poetry, ironically before and after the development of the microscope. And as late as the early nineteenth century, Hoffman used Leuvenhoek himself as a character in one of the Tales of Hoffman. The simple draper was depicted as a wizard who enslaved the Master Flea, whose magic lens looked into the hearts and minds of anyone who placed it on their eye. Even then the world of the microscopic and its mysteries which unfolded through the lens had a supernatural quality about it that continued to inspire wonder.

Blaise Pascal reflected upon this wonder in one of his Pensées where he spoke of the infinitely large, that is the universe, open to us by means of the telescope and the infinitely small, open to us through the development of the microscope. He wrote:

> For, after all, what is man in nature? A nothing compared to the infinite, a whole compared to the nothing, a middle point between all and nothing, infinitely remote from an understanding of the extremes; the end of things and their principles are unattainably hidden from him in impenetrable secrecy.

Equally incapable of seeing the nothingness from which he emerges and the infinity in which he is engulfed (Krailsheimer 1966).

Pascal understood that the lens which aids our sight has limitations. Even modern electron microscopy has a limit to its resolution, a limit to the truth it can unfold. So the lens is also a metaphor for our theological understanding of God. Our imperfect theologizing cannot perfectly clarify for us the truths of revelation. Like the limitations of glass lenses, or electron lenses or gravitational lenses, the lens of theology is only as good as the quality of human intellectual constructs that we use to attempt to understand the faith. Theology must leap beyond that lack of visual clarity through prayer to the ultimate truth which finds its origin in the nothingness from which we came and finds its goal in the infinity that surrounds us, of which we are only partially aware. Between the infinitely small and the infinitely large there lies all knowledge available to us, but not infinite knowledge possessed by God. We must be humble and realize that the Truth of God is ultimately beyond our efforts. At the same time we must never cease the search.

From this it can be argued that, as a result of the efforts of the early modern scientists during the Baroque, the lens helped bring to human consciousness how infinite infinity really was. With microscopes, we saw that the limit of the small was far greater that had been imagined. And once we saw tiny creatures, thinkers like Pascal envisaged worlds existing at that level approaching the infinity of nothingness.

At the other end of the size spectrum was a universe far vaster than ever imagined. In fact, both extremes re–defined material reality beyond the sphere of earth to encompass the near–infinite cosmos which pointed to the infinity of God. The revelation of God through the created order as distinct from the revelation gifted to us in the Incarnation has subsequently proved to be a nearly infinite source of the new.

WORKS CITED

Boorstin, Daniel J. *The Discoverers*. New York: Vintage Books, 1985.

Ford, Brian J. *Single Lens*. New York: Harper & Row, 1985.

Pascal, Blaise. *Pensées*. Trans. Alban J. Krailsheimer. Harmondsworth, England: Penguin,1966.

Mason, Stephen F. *A History of the Sciences*. New York: Collier Books, 1962.

Ronchi, Vasco "The influence of the early development of optics on science and philosophy." *Galileo: Man of Science*. Ed. McMullin Ernan. New York: Basic Books, 1967. 195-206.

Elmar J. Kremer

Jansenism

ABSTRACT. The important movement in seventeenth-century French Catholicism known as Jansenism is now much maligned but little understood. It included both a theological position on the relation of divine providence, grace and human free will, and a moral theology and position on sacramental practice. I am concerned only with the Jansenist position of providence, grace and free will. The essential Jansenist doctrine was accepted and defended especially by Antoine Arnauld and Blaise Pascal. It was also accepted, I argue, by Nicholas Malebranche. I argue that the works of these great Jansenists still have something to contribute to the unsettled question of the relation between grace and free will.

The Protestant Reformation and the Catholic Counter-Reformation are undeniably central to the transition from medieval to modern Europe that took place during the Baroque Period. And central to the Protestant revolt and the Catholic reaction is the topic of grace and free will.[1] But the disputes about grace and free will that dominated sixteenth and seventeenth century theology were not only between Catholics and Protestants, but also among rival Catholic positions. One of these was Jansenism. Jansenism was, of course, a Catholic position that was eventually rejected by the Church. Indeed many later Catholic theologians have made it their business to stay as far away from Jansenism as possible. But there is always the danger that a general movement in theology away from a position will go too far and lead to excesses of its own. For this reason, I suggest that we revisit Jansenism and try to develop an understanding of it that is more

[1] Luther says, "Regarding the other articles, the papacy, councils, indulgences and other minor details, one could tolerate the pettiness and silliness of the pope and his followers. But of all my doctrines this [his denial of freedom] is the most important" (*Assertion of all the articles of Martin Luther condemned by the latest Bull of Leo X*, 1521. In *Dictionnaire de Theologie Catholique*, vol. 9, col 1285).

Going for Baroque: Cultural Transformations1550-1650.
A St. Michael's College Symposium. Francesco Guardiani ed. Ottawa: Legas, 1999

accurate than the harsh caricatures found in most recent treatments of the movement.

I begin with a brief sketch of the context in which Jansen's *Augustinus* appeared, in 1640, about two years after his death. In this work, Jansen attempts to resolve the central question left unanswered by the *Congregationes de Auxiliis*, a series of *ad hoc* committees of Cardinals created to deal with a fierce controversy between the Jesuits and the Dominicans about grace, free will, and predestination. The dispute, the occasion for which was a work by the Jesuit Luis de Molina, took place against the background of the Council of Trent's reaffirmation of human free will against the Protestant reformers, especially Luther.[2]

Against Luther, the Council declared that free will is not destroyed by original sin and that when a human being receives grace and cooperates with it, he cooperates freely. But the Council did not put an end to dispute about grace and free will. In particular, it did not settle the question of whether human free will is independent of God, and in particular whether the free cooperation of a human being with grace is brought about by the grace or is independent of it. Molina took the position that God has a causal role in the occurrence of every free human choice, but that God's contribution never determines what choice is made. In Freddoso's words, God is an "indeterministic cause" of human free choices (de Molina, "Introduction" 19). So, for Molina, if a human being cooperates freely with grace, he does so by an act that is independent of the grace. In 1588, Molina published his *Concordia Liberi Abitrii cum Gratiae Donis, Divina Praescientia, Providentia, Praedestinone et Reprobatione ad Nonnullos Primae Partis Divi Thomae Articulos* (The Agreement of Free Will with the Gift of Grace, Divine Foreknowledge, Providence, Predestination and

---

[2] Canons 4 and 5 of Trent's Decree on Justification are directly relevant to my topic: 4. If anyone shall say that man's free will, moved and aroused by God, when he assents to God who excites and calls him, does not cooperate in such a way as to add anything to his disposition and preparation for obtaining the grace of justification, and that he cannot dissent if he wants, but that, like something inanimate, does nothing whatever and is merely passive, anathema sit. 5. If anyone shall say that after Adam's sin man's free will is lost and destroyed, or that it is a thing in name only, indeed a name without a corresponding reality, a fiction introduced into the Church by Satan, anathema sit (*Decrees of the Ecumenical Councils*).

Reprobation according to several articles in the First Part of St. Thomas). In this work, Molina tried to reconcile his position on human free will with Aquinas's position on grace, divine foreknowledge, and predestination.

Given Molina's position on human free will, and the Council of Trent's declaration that when a human being cooperates with grace, he does so freely, it follows that the grace of Christ, given to any fallen human being, does not by itself produce salvation, or indeed to any good work. Grace is efficacious, Molina says, only if the person who receives it cooperates by an act of free will that is not determined by the grace. Nevertheless, if anyone cooperates with grace, then God knew from all eternity that they would cooperate, and their cooperation was part of God's providence or His plan for the created universe, which is complete in every detail and includes everything that ever has happened, is happening or will happen. If a person not only cooperates with grace, but perseveres in his cooperation and is saved, then the person was predestined to salvation, that is, the person is one of the elect, whose salvation is part of God's eternal providence.

The key to Molina's reconciliation of these apparently conflicting doctrines is his claim that God has "middle knowledge" of what choice, if any, a human being would make in any possible circumstance. Consider an example given by the modern Molinist Alvin Plantinga:

> Curley Smith, the mayor of Boston, is opposed to the freeway route. . . . The Director of the Highways offers him a bribe of #35,000 to drop his opposition. Unwilling to break with the fine old traditions of Bay State politics, Curley accepts; whereupon the Director spends a sleepless night wondering whether he could have had Curley for $20,000.

In other words, Director asks himself which of the following propositions is true: (a) If Curley had been offered $20,000, he would have accepted the bribe; (b) If Curley had been offered $20,000 he would have rejected the bribe (*The Nature of Necessity* 173-74). According to Molina, either (a) or (b) is true, and God knows which one is true. Molina took this doctrine to imply that although created intelligences exercise free will independently of God, yet everything that happens in the created universe, down to the last detail, can be planned by God from all eternity. God's plan dictates, among other things, that all things work together for the good of those who, by their free, independent cooperation with grace, love God. Molina seems to hold that God chooses certain persons for salvation on the basis of His knowledge of how they would respond if offered the help of grace, and hence that predestination is not prior to the merits of those predestined. Molina's Jesuit confrere, Suarez, developed a version of the theory according to which God could bring it about that any human being is saved by supplying graces that He fore knew would be sufficient for that end. This allowed Suarez to return to the Augustinian and Thomistic position that predestination to salvation is prior to the personal merits of those who are predestined.

Molina's work was quickly and vigorously attacked by the more traditional Thomist, Domingo Bañez. Bañez was the leading Spanish Dominican theologian, and a figure of considerable stature in the Church. Among other distinctions, he was Theresa of Avila's confessor. Bañez not only held, like Molina, that all human acts of will are caused by God, but further that the free cooperation of a human being with the grace of Christ is caused by that grace. Molina's position, he thought, smacked of Pelagianism, since it implied that original sin so little affected the will that fallen man remained capable of contributing on his own to good works and hence to his own salvation. The dispute grew into a fight between the Jesuits and Dominicans, with the Franciscans playing a lesser role, and even the civil authorities became involved, the French on the Jesuits' side and the Spanish on the side of the side of the Dominicans. In response, Pope Clement VIII established the first of the *Congregationes de Auxiliis* to settle the matter. Both sides agreed that those who end up persevering in the love of God and hence are saved, are predestined for salvation as part of God's providence. They also agreed that the means whereby God carried out his providential plan for the predestined was grace, especially an actual, interior, supernatural grace whereby a person is moved and aroused to choose to act for the love of God for His own sake and above all other things. They agreed, finally, that actual grace infallibly has the good result that it was intended by God to have as part of His plan. But they disagreed about the way in which grace contributes to the accomplishment of the plan. The disagreement is described by Paul V, in the statement that concluded the *Congregationes*, in these words, "The difficulty is to know whether God moves the will physically or morally." Bañez expresses the difference as follows:

> [The Molinists say that] God is only a moral cause [of free choice], offering certain supernatural helps, which are sufficient if free choice wills to use them. But this good use is not really brought about by the causality of God's grace; it is brought about only morally, that is, only in so far as God at that time gives what He fore knew free choice would consent to. (*Tractatus*, vol. 3, 382)

As Molina puts it, the Bañezians hold that actual grace is a "physical premotion," which "by its very nature" produces a meritorious act,[3] but in truth actual grace is a stirring in the will such that whether it is efficacious "depends on whether or not the faculty of choice that is moved and stirred by [the grace] wills to consent to it and cooperate with it."[4] Both Bañezians and Molinists agree that actual grace is "infallibly" efficacious; but Bañezians hold that it is efficacious through itself, while Molinists hold that its efficacy depends on the recipient's free cooperation, which is independent of the grace, though foreknown by God.

The meetings began on January 2, 1598, but had not come to any decision at the time of Clement VIII's death, on March 5, 1605. His successor, Leo XI, lived only a few months after his election, and when he was in turn replaced by Paul V, the new pope decided to re-

---

3. Bañez's notion of a physical premotion is rather elusive. By it he refers to the initiation by God of a finite cause's action. Actual grace is not the only sort of physical premotion in the Bañezian scheme; physical premotions are found whenever a created thing acts causally, either causing its own acts or causing something to occur in another. In either event, the created, "secondary" cause acts under the influence of God, the "primary" cause, whose influence takes the form of a physical premotion in the created cause. According to Bañez, actual grace is a supernatural physical premotion occurring in the will and enabling it to elicit acts that go beyond the natural power of any rational creature. But it is not entirely clear whether he thinks that it is a reality in the finite cause distinct from the action of the cause. (See, for example, *Tractatus* 384).

4. In Alfred Freddoso's translation of Molina (203). Freddoso takes this to mean that actual grace "endows a free agent with a causal tendency, more specifically, a tendency toward choosing the good" (64).

convene the Cardinals and to press for a quick resolution. But his hopes were not realized, and in the end he terminated the *Congregationes*, without any resolution of the issue, on August 28, 1607 (the feast day of St. Augustine). Paul V closed the Congregations with the statement that both the Molinist and the Bañezian positions were consistent with the Council of Trent, and with the admonition that those present should "return home, and keep secret what was said and done."[5] A few years later he forbade further publication on the issues, even in the form of commentaries on St. Thomas. But his ruling, repeated some fifteen years later by Urban VIII, did not stop the controversy.

Thus Jansen's *Augustinus* was part of a controversy that had begun over fifty years earlier. What Jansen tries to do in the work is to settle the question that the *Congregationes de Auxiliis* had failed to resolve, and to settle it on the basis of principles drawn from St. Augustine. Like Bañez, Jansen emphasizes the claim that actual grace is efficacious *per se*. But Jansen distinguishes his position from that of the Dominicans in two ways: First, he says that actual grace is not an obscure "physical premotion" of the will, but rather a consciously experienced inspiration of the love of God, which is such that the one who receives it infallibly, though freely, consents to it. Second, he says that the first parents, Adam and Eve, as well as those who belong to the body of Christ, received actual grace. But the grace received by Adam and Eve was such as to require their independent, free cooperation in order to become a meritorious love of God, a cooperation

5. The central issue in dispute is pinpointed by Paul V in the statement with which he closed the *Congregationes*: "The Council of Trent defined the necessity of a divine motion for free will. The difficulty is to know whether God moves the will physically or morally. No doubt it would be desirable that controversy on the subject be terminated, but it is not necessary. Indeed, the opinion of the Order of Preachers is far from Calvinism, since they say that grace does not destroy but rather perfects freedom and that it makes man act according to his nature, that is, freely; on the other hand the Jesuits are distinct from the Pelagians in that the latter say that the point of departure of salvation comes from us while the former say the opposite. Since it is not necessary to come to a definition, the matter can be postponed to a more suitable time. If anyone teaches errors, the Holy Office exists and can oppose them. Let the members of the tribunal and the auditors, then, return home, and keep secret what was said and done" (*Dictionnaire de Théologie Catholique*, article on "Molinism," column 2165).

that was, of course, not forthcoming. By contrast, the grace of Christ is efficacious *per se*. Thus Jansen agreed with the Molinists about the grace received by Adam and Eve and the angels; but he agreed with Bañez about the grace of Christ, the grace that is appropriate for fallen man. He reaffirms the doctrine that all those who are saved are predestined to salvation prior to any personal merit, and says that efficacious grace is God's means for bringing about the good works and the salvation of fallen human beings in accordance with His providential plan. But he is careful to deny that anyone is predestined to sin, for it is not God's intention that anyone should sin. Nonetheless, the sins that occur, including the sin of Adam, are taken account of in God's plan, and it is God's intention that those who sin and do not repent should be punished.

The *Augustinus* was immediately attacked, among others by the official theologian of Paris, Isaac Habert, and then defended by a number of theologians connected with the monastery of Port-Royal, most importantly Antoine Arnauld, Pierre Nicole and Blaise Pascal. The Oratorian Nicolas Malebranche was also favorably impressed with the work.[6] But the Jesuits brought their complaints about the book to Rome and eventually Rome condemned a famous set of five propositions, which Rome claimed were in the *Augustinus*.[7] Pope Innocent X repudiated the five propositions in 1653, and the repudiation was repeated shortly afterwards by his successor, Alexander VII. Arnauld

6. Both Malebranche and Arnauld later rejected important parts of the Jansenist position. I discuss these matters in "Grace and Free Will in Arnauld," in "L'Accord de la grâce avec la liberté selon Arnauld," and in "Malebranche on Human Freedom," forthcoming in Stephen Nadler, editor, *The Cambridge Companion to Malebranche*.

7. The five propositions condemned in their Jansenist sense by Pope Innocent X in 1653 are: 1. Some of God's commandments are impossible for just men, even though they want to fulfill them and try to do so with their existing powers; and the grace which would make them possible is also lacking. 2. In the state of fallen nature there is never any resistance to interior grace. 3. In the state of fallen nature freedom from necessity is not required in man for merit or demerit but only freedom from constraint. 4. The semi-Pelagians admitted the necessity of antecedent interior grace for individual actions, even for the beginning of faith; they were heretical in holding that grace is such that the human will can resist it or comply with it. 5. It is semi-Pelagian to say that Christ died or shed his blood for each and every man.

and Nicole agreed that the propositions, as they would normally interpreted, when given without any context, are heretical, but pointed out that none of them are *verbatim* in Jansen's book.[8] Pascal, perhaps more forthrightly, said that the Pope meant to condemn these propositions precisely in the sense in which Jansen might have accepted them, and therefore that the Pope also condemned the doctrine of St. Augustine and of St. Paul.[9] A number of important Catholic figures agreed with the Jesuit attack on Jansenism, including St. Vincent de Paul and Jean-Jacques Olier, the head of the Sulpicians at Paris. Jansenism was no longer a viable position in the Church.[10]

But not only was Jansenism rejected, it was, to use a popular term, demonized. The description of Jansen's position given in the fifty-eighth edition Drioux's *Précis Elémentaire d'Histoire ecclésieastique* (Paris, 1909), is typical of the accounts given in theological manuals. Drioux gives an inexact list of the five condemned propositions and then adds, "This makes God a tyrant who orders the impossible, and man a machine who turns necessarily to the good when he has grace and to evil when he does not have it" (p. 227). This account is an unfair caricature of Jansen's position. I set aside the complex matter of the relation of the five condemned propositions to Jansen, and consider only the charge that Jansen makes God a tyrant and man a machine. Jansen holds that God's commands are all within our power to carry out, and that were it not for original sin there would be no obstacle to our carrying them out. Like Augustine and Aquinas before him, Jansen holds that if a person's sinful condition ensures that he will not obey some commandment of God, that does not excuse the person from guilt. Nor is it fair to say that Jansen makes man a machine. Jansen strove mightily to show that his position was consistent with the attribution of genuine freedom to human

---

8. More specifically, Arnauld pointed out that only the first proposition is composed of expressions found in Jansen's book. The other four bear no clear relation to Jansen's words. (*Réponse au P. Annat*, vol. 19, 151 ff.)

9. "There is no difference between condemning the doctrine of Jansen on the five propositions and condemning efficacious grace, St. Augustine, and St. Paul" (*Oeuvres de Blaise Pascal*, Vol. 10, 171).

10. For a detailed, scholarly discussion of the controversy about the five "Jansenist" propositions, see Bruno Neveu's *L'Erreur et son juge*.

beings, and held that whether human beings cooperate with grace or sin, they act *spontaneously*.[11] This spontaneity, he held, makes their good actions meritorious and their bad actions demeritorious. In sum, Jansen tried to show that it does not follow from his position that human beings are not machine-like and are not deprived of freedom.[12] There may be flaws in Jansen's argument, but it is hardly fair to simply declare that his position "makes man a machine." A reasonably sympathetic reading of the *Augustinus* shows that, though it contains important errors, it does not put forward the horrifying position so often attributed to its author.

I said at the outset that it would be worthwhile to reappraise Jansenism because the extreme reaction of Catholics against that position may well lead to errors opposite to those of Jansen. It has indeed become widespread among Catholics to reject Jansenism and everything associated with it, including many of the positions Jansen had in common with Molina and Bañez, and indeed with Augustine and Aquinas. In place of the doctrine of grace as a sure way by which God can carry out His detailed providential plan, modern Catholics tend toward the position that is called, in the literature in philosophy of religion, "free will theism." According to this position, when God creates a human being and allows him or her to make a morally significant free choice, then God *takes a risk*. The person may freely reject God, and there is nothing God can do about it. Nor is this approach confined to professional philosophers and theologians. I have come across a prayer by a modern Jesuit, John Powers, that contains this stanza:

> I affirm God as Courage,
> the mighty and first eternal risk-taker,

---

11. Jansen says that for an act to be "in the power [of the agent], and, in opposition to being subject to necessity of coercion, to flow spontaneously (*sponte*) from that power . . . is according to Augustine the true and genuine and natural notion of freedom" (*Augustinus*, Vol. 3, Bk. 7, Ch. 6, 315a).

12. Arnauld argued that Jansen was "surely mistaken" both about the nature of actual grace and about freedom of will. Arnauld developed his own position on both topics, derived from his reading of Aquinas and of Thomistic authors, including Estius. See n. 6 above.

who dares create me free enough to
reject even divinity.

But professional theologians and philosophers are more likely than others to test the implications of such approach. Thus the philosopher William Hasker goes so far as to suggest that God takes a risk that His entire purpose as a creator should be frustrated: "If every single human being has it in her power to accept or reject God's offer of salvation, and if God has no advance knowledge of how a person will respond, then it would be possible for every person without exception to reject salvation--and if this were to occur, there would be no "people of God," no Church, and a key element in God's plan would be frustrated" (103). Hasker consoles himself with the thought that this sort of frustration of God's will is extremely unlikely, though possible. God needs "luck" in order to fulfill His plan, but not much luck!

Hasker's argument is not sound. Even if it were true that whenever a human being is allowed by God to make a morally significant choice, God runs the risk that the human being will make a bad choice, it does not follow that God runs the risk that all human beings will reject salvation. Consider this analogy: From the premise that there is some risk that any given child will be less healthy than average, it does not follow that there is some risk that all children will be less healthy than average. But even if we can avoid Hasker's extreme conclusion about God's risks in allowing human being to make morally significant free choices, it seems to me that free will theism is theologically unacceptable. Consider the language of Pius IX's *Ineffabilis Deus*, in which he defined the Immaculate Conception of Mary: "The Most Blessed Virgin Mary from the first moment of her conception was by the singular grace and privilege of Almighty God, in view of the merits of Christ Jesus the Saviour of the human race, preserved immune from all state of original sin." Now Mary's agreeing to be the mother of Christ Jesus was a free act on her part, so according to free will theism, God ran the risk that Mary would not accept that role. How then could she have been given the privilege of being conceived free of original sin "in view of the merits of Christ Jesus"? For if, more than a decade later, she had rejected the offer to be the mother of Jesus, there would have been no such merits! It is implied by the Catholic doctrine that though Mary was free to decline the offer to be the mother of Jesus, God did not run any risk that she would do so.

This implication is recognized in the opening sentences of the encyclical:

> The ineffable God, whose ways are mercy and truth, whose will is omnipotent, and whose wisdom reaches mightily from end to end and gently (*suaviter*) disposes all things, from all eternity foresaw the deplorable ruin which would result for the human race from the transgression of Adam; and in an ever hidden mystery resolved to accomplish the first work of his goodness by a mystery even more profound, through the incarnation of the Word . . . He therefore, from the beginning and before all time, elected and ordained the mother from whom his son, having become incarnate, would be born.

Perhaps, then, we should go back and reexamine the theories of Molina, Bañez and Jansen. The exercise might help us to arrive at a more satisfactory position than that of the free will theists.

Works Cited

Arnauld, Antoine. *Réponse au P. Annat.* In *Oeuvres de Messire Antoine Arnauld.* Eds. Gilbert Du Pac de Bellegarde and Jean Hautefage. 43 volumes. Paris–Lausanne: Sigismond D'Arnay et Cie, 1775-83.

Bañez, Domingo. *Tractatus de Vera et Legitima Concordia Liberi Arbitrii Creati cum Auxiliis Gratiae Dei Efficaciter Moventis Humanam Voluntatem*, in *Commentarios Inéditos a la Prima Secundae de Santo Tomàs.* Ed. R. P. Vincente Beltran de Heredia, O. P. *The Cambridge Companion to Malebranche.* Madrid: Consejo Superior de Investigaciones Cientificas, 1948.

de Molina, Luis. *On Divine Foreknowledge.* Part IV of the *Concordia*, Translated, with an Introduction and Notes, by Alfred J. Freddoso. Ithaca: Cornell UP, 1988.

Decrees of the Ecumenical Councils. Ed. Norman P. Tanner. London: Sheed & Ward, 1990.

Dictionnaire de Théologie Catholique. Paris: Letouzey et Ane, 1903-50 [i.e. 1899-1950].

Hasker, William "Providence and Evil: Three Theories," *Religious Studies*, 28(1992): 91-105.

Jansenius, Cornelius. *Augustinus.* Rothomagi: Sumptibus Ioannis Berthelin, 1643.

Kremer, Elmar J. "Grace and Free Will in Arnauld." *The Great Arnauld and Some of His Philosophical Correspondents.* Ed. Elmar J. Kremer. Toronto: U of Toronto P, 1994. 219-239.

_________. Kremer, Elmar J. "L'Accord de la grâce avec la liberté selon Arnauld." *Chroniques de Port–Royal.* Paris: Bibliothèque Mazarine 44 (1995): 145-161.

_________. "Malebranche on Human Freedom," forthcoming in *The Cambridge Companion to Malebranche* . Ed. Stephen Nadler.

Neveu, Bruno. *L'Erreur et son juge.* Naples: Bibliopolis, 1993.

Pascal, Blaise. "*Ecrit sur la signature.* In *Oeuvres de Blaise Pascal.* Eds. Léon Brunschwicg, Pierre Boutroux and Félix Gazier. Paris: Librairie Hachette et Cie, 1914.

Plantinga, Alvin. *The Nature of Necessity.* Oxford: Clarendon Press, 1974.

Giulio Silano

Paolo Sarpi and Canon Law

ABSTRACT. A new consensus appears to be emerging among historians regarding the long controverted figure of Paolo Sarpi, priest, theologian, consultor in jure of the Venetian Republic, and possibly an atheist. This immensely talented man, perhaps in a disguised defense of the rights of private conscience, made his most useful and lasting contribution to the burning debates of his day by battling against the Roman Curia on behalf of Venice. Of necessity, given the nature of the disputes in which he was engaged, the canons were the weapons to which he most frequently had recourse. Can one discern his attitude to the canonical tradition? How does he present the connection between canon law and the historic constitution of the Church? How do his views on these matters fit within the view of Sarpi as the quintessential 'good dissimulator'?

If one were sufficiently odd, one could very well propose the view that the great changes of the sixteenth century were chiefly the result of the long festering envy which theologians felt toward canon law. Coming as they do after the successful revolt of the theologians, our potted histories of the Middle Ages too glibly have us think of the period as that of Anselm, Abelard, Bonaventure, Thomas. Without wishing to belittle the achievements of these great men, and perhaps being odd, I suggest to you that even they were relatively marginal to the life of the medieval Church and society. The case was entirely otherwise for Gratian, Huguccio, Sinibaldo Fieschi, Johannes Andreae. That this should seem to you a this string of unfamiliar names, I take as proof that history is written by the victors.[1]

[1] For a brief introduction to the history of canon law, and to its centrality in the history of the Middle Ages and beyond, see: James A. Brundage, *Medieval Canon Law*. The best introduction to canonical jurisprudence, at which Sarpi was to play for a very long time, remains: Gabriel Le Bras *et al. L'âge classique, 1140-1378: Sources et théories du droit*. An interesting introduction to select problems addressed by canon law and jurisprudence is provided by Richard H. Helmholz, *The Spirit of Classical Canon Law*. A spir-

Going for Baroque: Cultural Transformations1550-1650.
A St. Michael's College Symposium. Francesco Guardiani ed. Ottawa: Legas, 1999

If I had to single out one trait that most characterizes the Western Church through the several centuries that precede the sixteenth, it would be the conviction that the 'vulgo assai rozzo e indisciplinato,' the rough and undisciplined populace of whom we heard Galileo speak,[2] is capable of having its roughness somewhat smoothed and that it can fruitfully be subjected to much healthful discipline. Furthermore, the conviction was firm that law, particularly the Church's law, was the principal instrument by which to achieve these great ends.

What followed from this view was the birth and efflorescence of Western jurisprudence - an achievement centred primarily on Bologna and brought to fruition primarily by Italian jurists in cooperation with the Papacy. To them we owe the grand and fruitful effort to produce a wonderfully creative synthesis of the Roman and Christian legal traditions. From this synthesis are derived many of our legal doctrines and institutions.

ited and very readable account of canon law, in a form and with conclusions that Sarpi would have found abhorrent, but not necessarily surprising, is: Harold Berman, *Law and Revolution: The Formation of the Western Legal Tradition*. Other presentations of canon law, which clarify its role in, and links to, the broader Western juridical culture, include: Manlio Bellomo, *The Common Legal Past of Europe, 1000-1800,* and Ennio Cortese, *Il rinascimento giuridico medievale*. For a brief, and perhaps odd, view of the development of the Pope's role as supreme law-maker, see: Giulio Silano, "Of Sleep and Sleeplessness: The Papacy and Law, 1150-1300." As for the theologians' resentment of canon lawyers, its history is usefully canvassed, within an article which is not otherwise notable for its insights regarding medieval canon law, by G.H.M. Posthumus Meyjes, "Exponents of Sovereignty: Canonists as Seen by Theologians in the Late Middle Ages." For the relationship of this resentment to the very structures of academic formation, see: Yves M-J. Congar, "Un témoignage des désaccords entre canonistes et théologiens." Of course, teologians were not the only critics of the importance that lawyers came to occupy in the Church and in Christian society as a whole; for this larger critical context, see: John W. Baldwin, "Critics of the Legal Profession: Peter the Chanter and His Circle;" Stephan G. Kuttner, "Dat Galienus Opes et Sanctio Justiniana;" in *Linguistic and Literary Studies in Honour of Helmut A. Hatzfeld,* repr. with original pagination in Kuttner, *History of Ideas and Doctrines of Canon Law in the Middle Ages.*

[2] See Domenico Pietropaolo, above, 37.

In the Church, the just reward extended to these mighty labourers in the Lord's vineyard was a virtual monopoly on all the more important, and lucrative, offices and benefices. Popes, bishops, archdeacons, canons, all were often drawn from the ranks of those who had spent some time with the *Corpus Juris Canonici*.[3] Interestingly, unlike theology, lecturing on this *Corpus*, at least in Italy, was open to lay people.[4]

The older part of the *Corpus* was the *Decretum*, a compilation of the first thousand years of Christian history put together around 1140 at Bologna by Gratian, a monk who, because of his achievement, is known as the father of the science of canon law.[5] The second part of the *Corpus* consisted of compilations of papal decretals or decisions, mostly published after the *Decretum*, to fill legislative lacunae which had become evident in the wake of Gratian's efforts and those of his followers.[6] The public burning of these decretals by Luther was an eloquent sign of a theologian's resentment of canon law.[7] It was also

[3] For a brief introduction to some of the principal students of medieval canon law, and their often illustrious careers outside the lecture hall, see: Brundage, *Medieval Canon Law*, 56-59, 206-230. The standard edition of the *Corpus* is: **Ae.** Friedberg, *Corpus Iuris Canonici*.

[4] The most famous lay teacher of canon law was Johannes Andreae, on whom see: Brundage, *Medieval Canon Law*, 58-59, 216-17; Stephan G. Kuttner, "Johannes Andreae and His Novella on the Decretals."

[5] On Gratian's seminal role in the formation of canonical science, there is a very large literature, but for a particularly temperate and balanced view, see: Stephan G. Kuttner, "The Father of the Science of Canon Law;" Kuttner, "Research on Gratian: Acta and Agenda," repr. in Kuttner, *Studies in the History of Medieval Canon Law*.

[6] On the formation of collections of papal decretals, most useful is the brief description in: Brundage, *Medieval Canon Law*, 53-57.

[7] According to Sarpi, Luther's burning of the papal decretals was a reaction to the burning of Luther's own works by the Universities of Cologne and Louvain in the wake of Leo X's publication of the Bull *Exsurge, Domine*, condemning Luther's teachings. Sarpi states: "Ma le università di Colonia e Lovanio, liete che per l'editto pontificio fosse dato colore al giudicio loro, abbrugiarono publicamente li libri di Lutero; il che fu causa che egli ancora in Vitemberga congregata tutta quella scola, con forma di giudicio publicamente facesse abbrugiare non solo la bolla di Leone, ma insieme anche le decretali pontificie, e poi con un longo manifesto, pubblicato in scritto, ren-

a sign, of course, that, unlike his Scholastic predecessors, he meant to make no effort to tune the two strings of theology and canon law. Harmony was not what he was looking for. A hope of salvation grounded in faith and works would require such an harmony, since works had long been the proper purview of canon law.[8] *Sola fide* means, among other things, that theology alone is important for salvation; as for civic conduct, secular law can look after it. But there is the twist that civic conduct now includes the external life of the Church. Which only goes to show how far theologians will go to get rid of competition!

And now to jump to another theologian, namely Sarpi.

Paolo Sarpi was an immensely gifted man. He was born in Venice in 1552, which does not forbid us to regard him as a contemporary of Galileo and Campanella.[9] In his teens, Sarpi, against the wishes of his family, decided to enter the Servite Order, within which he rose to high positions. Still in his teens, he held public disputations on theological and canonical matters. He was almost equally young when he was denounced to the Inquisition by a fellow Servite for holding that

desse conto al mondo di quell'azzione, notando il papato di tirannide nella Chiesa, perversione della dottrina cristiana et usurpazione della potestà de' legitimi magistrati." *Istoria del Concilio Tridentino*, lib 1, *sub anno* 1520, which I cite from Sarpi's *Opere*, edited by. Gaetano and Luisa Cozzi (760), cited henceforth as Cozzi, *Opere*.

[8] For a charming and instructive introduction to the importance of the notion of harmony in the work of the medieval canonists, see: Stephan G. Kuttner, *Harmony from Dissonance: An Interpretation of Medieval Canon Law*.

[9] The most useful and accessible biography of Sarpi is to be found in the several Introductory Notes prefixed to selections from Sarpi's works, in: Cozzi, *Opere*, where Sarpi's early life and formation is discussed at 3-37. The fundamental biography of Sarpi remains the panegyrical and coy work of his long-time collaborator, Fulgenzio Micanzio, *Vita del padre Paolo dell'ordine de' servi e teologo della Serenissima Republica di Venezia* (Leiden 1646); a more easily accessible edition of the *Vita* is in: P. Sarpi, *Istoria del Concilio Tridentino*, ed. C. Vivanti (Turin 1974). On the friendly relations between Sarpi and Galileo, see: Gaetano Cozzi, "Galileo Galilei, Paolo Sarpi e la società veneziana," in *Paolo Sarpi tra Venezia e l'Europa*. As for Campanella, it must be said that he did not share Galilei's favourable impression of Sarpi, instead referring to him as a 'pseudo-theologian' who had sold himself, for which see: Giovanni Getto, *Paolo Sarpi* (12).

the doctrine of the Trinity could not be drawn from the first chapter of Genesis (Cozzi, *Opere*, 4-5). Sarpi was absolved of the charge, but even in the fact that it was made we may detect hints of his critical attitude, of his openness to the consideration of all sorts of questions. This openness is confirmed by what we know of his scientific interests. His interest in optics was praised in Acquapendente's seminal treatise on the subject. Galileo too, whom Sarpi befriended throughout his years at Padua, had praise for Sarpi's mastery of mathematics (Cozzi, *Opere*, 11-12, 36-37). But it was in theology that Sarpi gained his doctorate in 1578. The Bible, the Fathers, ecclesiastical history, natural philosophy took up all the time he could spare from his growing responsibilities within the Order. In 1575-78, he taught philosophy in the Venice Servite convent. In 1579, still a very young man, he was elected Father Provincial of the Venetian Province, and then was promptly selected a member of a three-man commission meeting in Rome to revise the rules of the whole Order. He would once more be sent to Rome for an extended stay, in 1585-88 or 1589, to serve as Procurator for the Order.[10]

This meteoric career might lead one to conclude that Sarpi was made for the Servite Order, and it for him. But this does not appear to have been entirely the case. For all the fact that Sarpi would remain a Servite throughout his life, he does not seem to have been motivated by strong religious sentiments, either in joining the Order, or in remaining a member of it. He appears rather to have felt about it as a member of an Oxford College might about the institution which allows him to pursue his own intellectual interests.[11]

---

[10] Cozzi, *Opere*, 7-9, 15-19. Cozzi (19) concluded that Sarpi left Rome an unhappy man. For all the interesting experiences he had had while there, meeting many of the leading lights of the Roman Curia and some of the more interesting Jesuits (with some of whom, especially Robert Bellarmine, he would joust repeatedly in future years), he began to profess an intense dislike for the Curia and the disreputable means which he thought were required for success in it.

[11] Getto, *Paolo Sarpi*, 58-61, builds a strong case, resting squarely on Micanzio's evidence, that the possibility of the *otium* to study was what drew, and kept, Sarpi within the Servite Order. Getto's argument in this regard fits rather (too?) neatly with his over-all view that Sarpi is best understood as a driven and cool intellectual, who lacks almost all other kinds of engagement with humanity, apart from his compelling curiosity.

The same lack of religious sentiment, and the same desire to allow himself to enjoy unabashedly the pleasures of study, lead Sarpi to petition the Venetian government to obtain a bishopric for him. As a member of a mendicant Order with few requirements, a poor bishopric would have done for him, and would have required little of him. And so, in 1600, the Venetian government sought for him the bishopric of Caorle. The Pope turned the request down. In 1601, having again applied, he was turned down for the bishopric of Nona, in Dalmatia; the reason given was that his opinions and his company were both suspect . He stopped applying.[12]

In 1605, relations between Venice and the Papacy became tense because Venice had promulgated laws which, in the Pope's view, unduly limited ecclesiastical freedom. On 28 January 1606, perhaps in preparation for the fight that was obviously coming, Sarpi was named consultor in jure of the Republic. Early in the same year, an interdict was decreed against Venice. Sarpi quickly composed a number of tracts that queried the validity and binding nature of the papal actions. He himself was summoned to appear in Rome. He sent a response which denied the validity of the citation. He was eventually excommunicated.[13] Far from seeking absolution, he would eventually be buried with the decree of excommunication in his hands, as if to seek admission to Heaven by its means.[14]

[12] For the tenor of Sarpi's petition to the government, see Cozzi, *Opere*, 27. Getto, *Paolo Sarpi*, 74-75, stresses how Sarpi's petition reveals no interest whatsoever in undertaking the responsibilities that ought to go with the episcopal office. The initiative to seek nomination to the office is Sarpi's own; the clear definition of the office as one meant to allow him to study, in the service of the Republic, is also his own.

[13] A lucid summary of all these events, with a clear presentation of Sarpi's reaction and his initial efforts on behalf of the Republic, is in: Cozzi, *Opere,* 113-28. The most compelling account in English of these events, with an analysis of their importance within the longer history of Venetian-papal relations, and a fascinating discussion of their meaning for Venetian self-definition, is still: W.J. Bowsma, *Venice and the Defence of Republican Liberty: Renaissance Values in the Age of Counter-Reformation*.

[14] Sarpi was excommunicated personally on 5 January 1607, he kept the text of the decree among his papers and was buried with it: Vittorio Frajese, 15.

It is most interesting that the Republic of Venice, in seeking a legal advisor in its resistance to papal censure, should have gone to Sarpi, a doctor of theology. Why should it have done so?

Perhaps some of the reasons are suggested by Sarpi himself in a letter which he wrote to the Gallican jurist, Jacques Leschassier, on 13 May 1608. Leschassier had been at work on the edition of an ancient collection of canon law, but was doubtful as to whether he should publish it because its contents contained texts that seemed to justify claims to papal jurisdiction over other bishops. Sarpi encouraged him to go ahead because he thought the difficulties could be disposed of in a manner that would show that papal claims were ill-founded. He agreed too that the publication of books is insufficient. The education of youth in sound sentiments is more important. And he bemoaned how little such an education was available in Italy. The main cause of this lack, Sarpi suggested, was the conviction of Italian law professors, in their ignorance of history and chronology, that the Church had never been without papal decretals.[15]

Sarpi then recounted how, at the beginning of the dispute regarding the interdict, a meeting had been held with several professors to discuss the question of the exemption of clerics from secular jurisdiction, which was one of the subjects in contention with the Papacy. One of those present (Sarpi himself?) had stated that the liberty of the Republic, such as it was, was yet older than any papal decree exempting clerics from secular jurisdiction. But a Padua professor, amid the ap-

---

[15] Cf. *Sarpi's Lettere ai Gallicani,* 10-12: "Ex eo codice [Moguntino] ostendi poterit quam noviter auctoritas data fuerit decretalibus, quas Gratianus collegit, et quibus praecipue recens canonistarum doctrina innititur. Quod enim ad Sardicenses canones attinet, per multas editiones conciliorum iam vulgati sunt, neque desunt nobis quae ad eos respondeamus, licet pro maxime veris et indubitatis ac sinceris admiserimus. ... Bene mones (vir excellentissime) editionem librorum parum prodesse, longe vero praestare educationem iuventutis, et arcanum aperis, quod si nobis cordi et curae esset, ut deceret, ita res nostrae componerentur, ut nulli invidendum foret. Isthic parlamenta habetis seminaria sanae doctrinae; nobis nulla sunt. Professores nostri ita sunt et historiae et chronologiae rudes, ut sint, qui putent ecclesiam sine decretalibus nunquam fuisse." Ulianich's whole Introduction to this volume (XIII-CXLV) is illuminating regarding Sarpi's relations with the lively and, to him, sympathetic group of Gallicans jurists; on Leschassier, see LXXII-LXXXIV.

plause of the rest, condemned this view. He held instead that it was heretical to say that the canons of the Roman pontiffs are recent because the Church has always been governed by them. A reply was made (again, perhaps by Sarpi himself?) pointing out that papal decrees all bear the name of their authors and that history tells us when each of them lived. The professor replied that it is a plague and a ruination of laws to want to have recourse to history. Lawyers ought to imitate the famous jurists, Bartholus and Baldus, who did not spend any time in historical study, and the study of the laws has been ruined since the moderns began to interpret them by recourse to history and latinity.[16]

I hope it is clear why I have recounted this story at such length. I believe it makes clear that the Republic chose Sarpi as its legal counsellor because it did not want advice from lawyers, but from someone who, like Luther, would have been willing to burn the *Corpus Juris Canonici*. For the story makes clear Sarpi's frustrated awareness that lawyers could not have said that the Republic was right in resisting papal authority. Everything in their texts, in their training, and in their inclination made for the conclusion that the pope was within his rights. The Paduan lawyers were wedded to the *ius commune* system,

[16] *Sarpi, Lettere ai Gallicani*, 12: "In ipso exordio praeteritarum controversiarum dum in loco valde celebri de clericorum exemptione in criminalibus ageretur, unus quidam dixit, huius reipublicae libertatem licet in exigua fortuna multo antiquiorem esse quibuscunque pontificiis decretis de clericorum exemptione. Quod exceptum ab uno ex patavinis professoribus, reliquis applaudentibus, hac censura notatum fuit: esse haereticam doctrinam putare canones romanorum pontificum novos esse, cum semper illis ecclesia gubernata fuerit. Cui cum obiceretur omnia decreta pontificum nominibus auctorum notari, scirique pariter ex historiis quo quisque tempore vixerit, neque quod verum est posse ab ullo damnari, respondit esse labem et pernitiem legum velle ad historias recurrere, imitandos esse potius celebres iurisconsultos Bartholum, Baldum et qui his studiis operam nullam insumpserunt, et legum professionem labefactatam postquam moderni aliqui voluerunt per historias et latinitatem leges interpretari. Quid vis amplius? In Italia iurisconsultorum multi nunquam collectionem Iustinianam vident, pauci legunt primos iurisconsultos nostrorum saeculorum, plurimi contenti sunt lectione recentiorum, qui nihil praeter allegationes congerunt, ut ille doctissimus censeatur qui plures allegare vel alligare potuerit. Erudiri iuventus non potest nisi ab eruditis magistris. Utinam sola negativa ignorantia laboraremus, et non illa prava et quae scientiam repellit."

within which the Papacy acted as a Supreme Court for all Christendom, and they treated papal decisions as lawyers treat the decisions of a court. Such decisions cannot be historicised, at least not without grave risk of a legal system falling apart. It is still common practice to regard court decisions, even those published this week, as if they expressed what had always been the law. To do otherwise would introduce extra-juridical considerations into the definition of the law and would make the law even more uncertain than it already is.

But, of course, that was exactly Sarpi's aim. The relatively conservative nature of the Venetian ruling class made it impossible simply to hold a bonfire. And so one was reduced to historicizing papal law in order to dismiss it as an innovation. Little did it matter that the 'innovation' might go back to before the foundation of the Venetian Republic. If this meant that canon law became uncertain, that was all to the good because, in Sarpi's view, canon law, as a body of jurisprudence which did not spring from the state, had no right to exist.

Not that this conclusion could easily have been deduced from Sarpi's public statements. Once more, the conservative nature of the Venetian regime, its conviction that changes in religion risked causing changes also in a political constitution to which they were profoundly attached, meant that even the boldest members of Venice's ruling class were not willing to move to a definitive breach with the Papacy and to the adoption of some version of a Protestant state church. And so Sarpi was compelled to take a more nuanced approach, or even several apparently contradictory approaches, toward law in his long service as legal counsellor to the Republic.[17]

Sarpi's most usual activity as consultor was to render opinions on issues of ecclesiastical policy as they arose. More than 900 such opinions survive in the Venetian archives. In these, Sarpi follows

---

[17] It is far from clear whether Sarpi himself was interested in a bonfire. It may be that the game was much more fun as he was playing it than as Luther had done. He was not averse from allowing his Protestant correspondents to believe that Venice might soon be ready to take radical steps away from Rome and in their direction, but, finally, this never seems to have looked probable, or even desirable, to him. The most elegant and convincing discussion of these issues is in Frajese, *Stato e Chiesa a Venezia* (256-75, 289-306, and *passim*); Frajese (129-36 and *passim*) is also most lucid on the peculiar Venetian approaches to law, which Sarpi fruitfully, and shamelessly, makes his own.

more or less the practices that were acceptable to the law professors. He cites from the *Corpus Juris Canonici*, both Decretum and decretals, as if they were binding. He treats as equally binding the glosses on these texts and the opinions of the commentators on them, both medieval and contemporary. But he is sparing in his citations. He avoids the piling up of authorities which his French correspondents find ludicrous in the Italian practice. And his conclusions never agree that the law is as the Papacy regards it. The form is saved. The terms and categories dear to the law professors are preserved. But the integrity of the jurisprudence is never allowed to stand in the way of the assertion of a greater and greater control on the part of theVenetian state over its ecclesiastics.[18]

It is a method of which he makes fun, even as he boasts about it. In another letter to Jacques Leschassier, of 27 April 1610, he explains that, in his anti-papal action, he is constrained. He cannot achieve all that he wishes, but neither is he without achievements. And he explains that some of his achievements are due to his having mastered

[18] A selection of the less typical opinions rendered by Sarpi is published in Cozzi, *Opere,* 468-634; the famous opinions regarding the inquisition and the rights of church immunity are in: P. Sarpi, *Scritti giurisdizionalistici*. In Cozzi, *Opere*, 464-67, is also to be found a text entitled, "Carico di consultor in iure della Republica, 15 settembre 1618," in which Sarpi, boasting somewhat of his achevements and in order to ensure continuity in the office, states his view of the function of counsellor in the following terms: "L'ufficio del consultor in iure è rispondere quel che è di raggione nel fatto o caso over negozio che gli vien proposto. Per rispondere *de iure* nelle scole non vi si ricerca altro che una buona cognizione delle legi perché li casi si propongono in termini universali che non ricevono varieta e quel che una volta è ben discuso serve per sempre. Ma a consultare nei casi particolari oltra la cognizione delle legi vi vuole esquisita notizia del fatto cioè del negozio con tutte le sue particolari circonstanze et è regola di giurisconsulti che qualonque minima variazione di circonstanza muta tutta la raggione *in iure*." In effect, here too, Sarpi ends up saying that the law professors do best to stick to abstractions. One cannot expect them to get their hands dirty in archives in order to find the *specific facts* of the case, but these facts may very well render the learned abstractions of the professors pointless. And so, in the same text, Sarpi goes on to enumerate a number of celebrated cases in which his investigation of the archives had made for the Republic's triumph, after celebrated juriconsults had, from their distant studies, offered learned opinions that did nothing to make for a resolution of these matters.

what the Italian lawyers mean when they speak of a text or gloss as famous. They do not mean that the text or gloss is clear; they do not adduce these texts in their true sense, but force them to bear an agreed meaning. If a sufficient number of teachers agree that a text can bear a meaning that is not obvious, then the interpretation is regarded as famous by the lawyers.[19]

Leschassier had compared this practice to that of theologians who misinterpret the words of Scripture. Sarpi begs to differ. Such theologians are mishandling what is not their own and the Word of God is to remain forver firm, so their offense is great. But jurists are mishandling what they themselves have produced. In any case, all laws are subject to custom, so it is not a problem that their interpretation is adapted to changing times and events. The Roman Curia provides a continuous example of this approach. It claims to respect the canons in their integrity, and yet interprets them to suit its interests. So what if the interpretation goes against the text? It does not matter. Even if one is not showing honour to the law, yet one is not inflicting public injury upon it![20]

---

[19] Sarpi, *Lettere ai Gallicani*, 76-77: "Sed vide quibus angustiis premar. Ea ratione mihi parcissime utendum; sicut enim ego firmare bonos usus volo, ita adversarii defendunt abusus. Ego id tento, ut beneficia indigenis tantum dentur, pensionibusque non graventur, quae duo in intolerandos abusus abiere, quos contra defendunt Romani, quoniam id actum a pontificibus, sciente, vidente neque contradicente principe, populo, et clero. Mihi non desunt sincerae ac verae rationes, quibus differentiam ostendam, quia lex naturalis consuetudine neque tolli neque minui potest. Non quantum vellem ago, neque tamen nihil facio. Quod a me petis de glosa, ubi possessorium spiritualium temporale esse dicatur, ego more italico loquutus sum. Nos dicimus saepe textum celebrem, aut glosam celebrem, non quia clara, sed quia frequentata, id est frequenter in eum sensum est allegata. Nostri iurisconsulti praesertim saeculi superioris, nunquam, aut fere nunquam, quicquam adducunt, quod si examines reperias in vero sensu allegatum; inde qui emunctioribus naribus praediti sunt, quoties communis opinio textum intelligit in sensu a vero alieno, non propterea ab eo allegando in eodem sensu desistunt, sed aiunt est textus celebris, id est quod frequenter a doctoribus in eo sensu allegatur, licet illi maxime sciant alienum esse a vero ..."

[20] Sarpi, *Lettere ai Gallicani*, 77: "Quod vero aequiparas doctores iuris theologis abutentibus sacrae scripturae locis, si mihi permiseris, dispari loco habendos dixero, et ut hos damnandos, ita illos excusandos. Theologos, in eum numerum pono, qui re aliena abutuntur, iurisconsultos in eorum qui sua: ver-

While making fun of the lawyers, Sarpi is here explaining his own method. While seeming to agree with the normative value of canon law, he feels justified to write as if he enjoyed the same freedom to interpret the laws as the supreme judge, or as the community of qualified interpreters of the law whose exegesis is subject to verification by their colleagues. He is confident that, by the relentless production of opinions which bolster Venetian sovereignty, he is adapting the laws to times and circumstances. Indeed, he insists that his actions are directed to a restoration of things to the state in which they ought always to have been.

What is this original state? Simply put, it is one in which the Church could make no claim to an autonomous power to make laws.

Notice the precision of the claim. It is not that the Church cannot make laws. Obviously enough, the Church has been making laws for a long time, and princes have long accepted the Church's ability to do so. What Sarpi denies is that the Church makes law by divine right. It is not God who has empowered the Church to make laws, but the prince. Were it not so, a Christian society would be a two-headed monster without a clear locus of sovereignty. And so, what the prince has given, the prince can take away. This is not as good as a bonfire, but it is close enough.[21]

bum domini in aeternum manet, neque tolli ab hominibus potest, neque mutari; at iura consuetudini subiciuntur, quae sicut illa tollere potest, quid mirum, si commoda ac opportuna interpretatione tempori et rebus aptentur? Id me romana curia sapientior effecta, edocuit. Olim nihil illi frequentius quam revocatio, aut derogatio canonum et constitutionum, quod maximum contemptum ingeneravit. Modo apage ut id faciat, maxime illos veneratur, sed tamen interpretatione rebus suis accommodat. Ita de concilio Tridentino agitur. Quid vero si interpretatio sit contra textum ? Nihil ad rem; si reipsa honos non est exhibitus legi, attamen iniuria non est palam irrogata. Sed nimis in his nugis progredior. Ad rem redeo. ..."

[21] Sarpi to Jacques Gillot, Letter of 29 September, in: Sarpi, *Lettere ai Gallicani*, 136-138, at 137-38: "Cum ambae potestates, ecclesiastica et saecularis, ad eandem rempublicam christianam pertineant, necesse est vel alteram alteri, vel ambas alicui summae potestati humanae subesse, vel ipsam christianam rempublicam monstrum biceps fore. Cunctas nationes et urbes, populus, aut primores, aut singuli regunt: sine maiestate humana, nulla respublica vel consistet, vel stare poterit. Non est quod mihi Barclaius ad divinam maiestatem veluti in comoedia ad Deum ex machina recurrat, tum quia oportet maiestatem esse reipublicae partem, non externum aliquod, tum quia omnes

The claim is radical. It constitutes the rejection of the so-called Gelasian principle. This is the distinction which Pope Gelasius had drawn in the second half of the fifth century, at just about the time that people fleeing the Huns had made their way to the Venetian la-

---

mundi respublicae una essent, nempe subiectae Deo, cui non magis aut minus subest rex Francorum quam Turcarum aut Persarum. Vides rempublicam israeliticam, cum post Salomonem sub duabus potestatibus fuit, divisam etiam in respublicas duas, neque unitatem retinuisse sub duobus regibus. Mitto antiqua. Cur francicum et hispanicum regnum duo sunt, licet communem habeant Deum, cum utrumlibet maiestatem habeat sibi propriam, invicem non subiectas ? Neque si rempublicam instituas quae a duabus potestatibus regatur, licet sub Deo, illam diuturniorem facies, quam Roma sub duobus conditoribus. Igitur ecclesiastici et saeculares duae respublicae erunt, si potestas una alteri non subiciatur, vel ambae uni, quae in eadem republica reperiatur. Divina maiestas nullam praebebit unitatem. Hoc argumentum ego dissolvere minime possum. Rogo te caecitatem meam illustres et si quidem fallaciam vides, non est quod sequentia legas, quibus explicem meam, dicam potius opinionem vel suspicionem, quam sententiam. Arbitror ego regnum et ecclesiam duas respublicas esse, constantes tamen ex eiusdem hominibus, alteram prorsus caelestem, alteram terrenam omnino, easque subesse propriis maiestatibus, defendi armis et munitionibus propriis, nihil habere commune, neque unam alteri bellum ullo modo inferre posse. Cur enim arietari possent in eodem loco non ambulantes ? Christus dixit se ipsum et discipulos non esse de mundo, et quod est clarius, nec segniter perpendendum divus Paulus nostrum politeuma in caelis esse protestatur. Nunc ecclesiam accipio pro fidelium convocatione, non vero pro clericis solis; quod si pro his accipiatur, non est regnum Christi, sed est pars reipublicae terrenae, eaque subiecta maiestati, cui et saeculares subiciuntur. Ambiguitas subest huic vocabulo *ecclesiastica potestas*; si enim ea intelligatur, qua regnum Christi, regnum caelorum administratur, ea nulli temporalia subest, nulli imperat, ad aliam non potest arietari, praeterquam ad satanicam, cum qua assidue illi bellum; si vero qua disciplina clericorum regitur, ea non est potestas regni caelorum, ea pars est reipublicae. Ita sensisse videntur utriusque imperii imperatores regesque Gothorum et, omnium maxime, Iustinianus, neque Caroli Magni capitolare aliud innuit. Principes, qui clericos a magistratibus exemerunt, ansam illis tribuere, ut nacti desides reges, quod gratia donatum fuit, veluti debitum arriperetur, et iure divino vel saltem proprio ecclesiastico assereretur. Ego primus in Italia, nullo praeeunte, ausus sum dicere neminem principum exemisse clericos a sua potestate sed a magistratuum subiectione..." Similar views are expressed in equally strong terms in a letter of Sarpi to Gillot of 8 December 1609, *ibid.*, 138-43.

goon. Writing to a Byzantine emperor, Gelasius asserted the co-existence in Christian society of the sacred authority of pontiffs and of the royal power. Both were God-given. The first was supreme over souls, the second over bodies. Because souls are more important than bodies, pontifical authority is more exalted than royal power.[22]

The Gelasian distinction is at the root of the Western tradition of distinguishing Church and state. It is also the most famous foundation for the assertion of an autonomous and God-given power for the Church to exercise jurisdiction over emperors, since they too have souls which can only be saved under the authority of pontiffs. To Sarpi, this is the source of all troubles and he emphatically denies it as an innovation which violates immemorial custom and the practice of the early Church.

Should Sarpi then be read as one who, having historicized more recent practices of the Church in order to dismiss them, wants, like the Protestant reformers, to return to a form of Christianity which is more faithful to its origins? No. Sarpi does not find the early Church particularly admirable. For him, the object of historical research into Christian origins does not involve the possibility of discovering a golden age that one might now try to retrieve. It is almost with glee that he points out that Judas was one of the apostles and that even the Church of Corinth, although established by no less a personage than St. Paul, was so quickly depraved that it had to be condemned by its very founder. If the Church is ever going to be perfect, it will be at the end of history, when Christ will come to make it perfect. Until then, it is best left in the hands of the state. It is for that reason that he resists all invitations to join any of the reformed churches. He has no greater trust that they will avoid depravity. So the only safe thing to do is to belong to the Church which your sovereign has approved, while trying to make sure that that same sovereign does not mistakenly surrender prerogatives which exclusively belong to him(Sarpi to Leschas-

[22] This foundational text is excerpted in Gratian's *Decretum*, D. 96 c. 10 (Vol. 1, c. 340, in Friedberg's edition of the *Corpus Iuris Canonici*), and its most salient portion reads as follows: "Duo sunt quippe, imperator auguste, quibus principaliter hic mundus regitur: auctoritas sacra Pontificum, et regalis potestas. In quibus tanto grauius est pondus sacerdotum, quanto etiam pro ipsis regibus hominum in diuino sunt reddituri examine rationem. § 1. Nosti itaque inter hec ex illorum te pendere iudicio, non illos ad tuam posse redigi uoluntatem."

sier, *Lettere ai Gallicani*, 90-93). This task is particularly demanding when confronting the effrontery of what he likes to call the *totatus*, the supposed claim of the papalists that the papacy is everything.[23] Resistance to this claim appears to have been the one great unifying cause of Sarpi's thought and action.

Even the claim that a prince might be tolerant of some Church autonomy because religious law helps to keep subjects obedient is denied by Sarpi, although not publically. In a collection of reflections on various subjects, which did not begin to be published until this century, he confronts the contention that the Torah helps to keep subjects honest, only to reject it. He contends that religious law is likely to check only subjects who are timid, and for these the state's law suffices.[24]

The picture of Sarpi that I have been drawing is a rather cheerless one. And indeed, apart from his over-indulgence in sarcasm against the Papacy and all its supporters, it is difficult to discern what might have given this theologian joy. And yet he has many admirers. His unrelenting work to move the Venetian state in the direction of be-

---

[23] On this happily malicious expression, which recurs frequently in Sarpi's correspondence and elsewhere in his works, see Boris Ulianich, *Paolo Sarpi. Lettere ai Gallicani*, LII and *passim*.

[24] Sarpi, *Pensieri filosofici,* 67: "413- Non è vero che la Tora ritenga le Repubbliche, e che senza lei non sosterrebbonsi; perciocché l'uomo è di natura timida o audace; se timida con altri terrori a sufficienza si tiene; se audace, a tenerlo non basta qual si voglia, benché fosse maggiore. Vedesi ciò, perché l'asprezza di tanti generi di morte, quantunque eccessive, gl'uomini feroci non ritengono. Quando però la Tora non fosse, i timidi per altre minacce temerebbono, e gli arditi nullameno sarebbon tali, sebbene ella vi fosse. E quantunque a noi paia che, se non fosse questa, faremmo cio' ed altro, nondimeno non e' vero, perche' talun che l'abbia deposta dal suo animo seguita co' medesimi costumi, senza peggioramento veruno. Anzi di due del medesimo temperamento e inclinazione, de' quali l'uno l'abbia e l'altro no, niuna differenza si conosce. Gran danno certamente della Repubblica sarebbe lasciar quella e gli altri terrori levare, ma poco, levar quella, gli altri lasciando...." Getto (*Paolo Sarpi*, 122-23) warns against making too much of reflections like this one, of which there are many in the mentioned collection. Although he takes these too to be evidence of Sarpi's unbounded curiosity, which extends its consideration to everything, he rightly stresses the fragmentary nature of these reflections; he refuses to regard them as definitive affirmations.

coming a modern state has found much praise. And Vittorio Frajese, in his recent and admirable study of Sarpi, has tried to find ideal motives for Sarpi's action. In part by accepting David Wootton's reading of Sarpi's *Pensieri*, Frajese agrees that Sarpi was probably an unbeliever, a moral atheist, who had come to find Christianity repugnant. Frajese then proceeds to argue that Sarpi's entire anti-papal action was directed to the creation of a space of freedom and autonomy for the individual where one would be free from the clutches of bodies like the Inquisition in order to pursue one's own private search for truth unhindered. It is true that this requires one's outward conformity with whatever religion the state has decided to endorse, or at least this will be required until the establishment of a secular society, indifferent to religion, as any decent society ought to be.[25]

This view of Sarpi finds some justification in his repeated insistence to his correspondents that, in the circumstances of his time, one had to wear a mask and was not free to say all one thought. I cannot say that I find the view entirely compelling. But neither do I have a better view to submit to you today, apart perhaps from the suggestion that Sarpi is among the first of the court theologians and one of the most impressive of them. The type is an original creation of the Baroque period. Whether these theologians are an effect or a cause of the epistomological uncertainty of the period I cannot say. But they did thrive in it and on it.

[25] Frajese, *Stato e Chiesa a Venezia*, esp. ch. 1, and *passim*; Frajese here accepts and, expands upon, the views of David Wootton. The effect of these views would be to make Sarpi, as it were, the first 'modern' thinker. Having already served as a great exemplar for Protestants, jurisdictional writers, anticlericals of various sorts, Italian nationalists, and so on, now Sarpi would go on to become the hero of self-fashioning and 'liberal' individualists.

WORKS CITED

Baldwin, John W. "Critics of the Legal Profession: Peter the Chanter and His Circle." *Proceedings of the Second International Congress of Medieval Canon Law*. Vatican City: S. Congregatio de Seminariis et Studiorum Universitatibus, 1965. 249-259. (Monumenta Iuris Canonici, Subsidia, vol. 1).

Bellomo, Manlio. *The Common Legal Past of Europe, 1000-1800.* Trans. Lydia G. Cochrane. Washington, D.C.: Catholic University of America, 1995.

Berman, Harold J[oseph]. *Law and Revolution: The Formation of the Western Legal Tradition.* Cambridge, MA: Harvard UP, 1983.

Bowsma, William James. *Venice and the Defence of Republican Liberty: Renaissance Values in the Age of Counter-Reformation.* Berkeley: U of California P, 1968.

Brundage, James A. *Medieval Canon Law.* London: Longman, 1995.

Congar, Yves M-J. "Un témoignage des désaccords entre canonistes et théologiens." *Études d'histoire du droit canonique dédiés à Gabriel Le Bras.* Paris: Sirey, 1965. Vol. 2, 861-84.

Cortese, Ennio. *Il rinascimento giuridico medievale*. Rome, 1992.

Cozzi, Gaetano. "Galileo Galilei, Paolo Sarpi e la società veneziana." *Paolo Sarpi tra Venezia e l'Europa*. Ed. G. Cozzi. Turin:Einaudi, 1979. 135-234.

Frajese, Vittorio. *Stato e Chiesa a Venezia tra Cinque e Seicento.* Bologna: Il Mulino, 1994.

Friedberg, A. *Corpus Iuris Canonici.* 2 vols. Leipzig 1879. Repr. Graz, Akademische Druck–U. Verlagsanstalt, 1959.

Getto, Giovanni. *Paolo Sarpi*. Firenze: Olschki, 1967.

Helmholz, Richard H. *The Spirit of Classical Canon Law.* Athens, GA: U of Georgia P, 1996.

Kuttner, Stephan G[eorg]. "Johannes Andreae and His Novella on the Decretals." *The Jurist* 24 (1964): 393-408.

__________. "Research on Gratian: Acta and Agenda." *Proceedings of the Seventh International Congress of Medieval Canon Law*. Ed. Peter Linehan. Vatican City: Biblioteca Apostolica Vaticana, 1988. (Monumenta Iuris Canonici, Subsidia, vol. 8). Repr. in Kuttner, *Studies in the History of Medieval Canon Law.* Aldershot [England]: Variorum / Brookfield, VT: Gower, 1990.

__________. "The Father of the Science of Canon Law." *The Jurist* 1 (1941): 2-19.

__________. *Harmony from Dissonance: An Interpretation of Medieval Canon Law.* Latrobe PA:Archabbey, 1960. (Wimmer Lectures, 10).

_________. "Dat Galienus Opes et Sanctio Justiniana." in *Linguistic and Literary Studies in Honour of Helmut A. Hatzfeld*. Ed. Alessandro S. Crisavulli. Washington, D.C.: Catholic U of America P, 1964. 237-56. Repr. with original pagination in Kuttner, Stephan G. *History of Ideas and Doctrines of Canon Law in the Middle Ages*. London: Variorum Reprints, 1992 (2d ed.).

Le Bras, Gabriel, and Charles Lefebvre, Jacqueline Rambaud. *L'âge classique, 1140-1378: Sources et théories du droit*. Histoire du droit et des institutions de l'Église en Occident, vol. 7. Paris: Sirey, 1965.

Meyjes, G.H.M. Posthumus. "Exponents of Sovereignty: Canonists as Seen by Theologians in the Late Middle Ages." *The Church and Sovereignty c. 590-1918. Essays in Honour of Michael Wilks*. Ed. Diana Wood. Oxford: Blackwell, 1991. 299-312. (Studies in Church History, Subsidia vol. 9).

Micanzio, Fulgenzio. *Vita del padre Paolo dell'ordine de' servi e teologo della Serenissima Republica di Venezia*. Leiden: [s.n.], 1646.

_________. *Vita del padre Paolo dell'ordine de' servi e teologo della Serenissima Republica di Venezia*. In Sarpi, Paolo. *Istoria del Concilio Tridentino*. Ed. C. Vivanti. Turin: Einaudi, 1974. Vol. 2, 1273-1413.

Sarpi, Paolo. *Istoria del Concilio Tridentino*. In *Opere*.

_________. *Lettere ai Gallicani*. Ed. Boris Ulianich. Wiesbaden: F. Steiner, 1961. (Veröffentlichungen des Instituts für Europäische Geschichte Mainz, Band 26).

_________. *Opere*. Eds. Gaetano and Luisa Cozzi. Milan and Naples: Ricciardi, 1969.

_________. *Pensieri filosofici e scientifici*. In *Opere*.

_________. *Scritti giurisdizionalistici*. Ed. Giovanni Gambarin. Bari: Laterza, 1958.

_________. "Of Sleep and Sleeplessness: The Papacy and Law, 1150-1300." *The Religious Role of the Papacy: Ideals and Realities*. Ed. Christopher Ryan. Toronto: Pontifical Institute of Medieval Studies, 1989.

Wootton, David. *Paolo Sarpi Between Renaissance and Enlightenment*. Cambridge: Cambridge UP, 1983.

Benoît Bolduc

The Shepherd's Baroque Nature

> Le baroque, attribut, comme on l'a dit parfois, de la culture des époques de transition? Non—mais du regard un peu affolé qu'une époque de transition peut jeter sur la culture.
>
> Pierre Charpentrat

> La pensée moderne s'est peut-être inventé le baroque comme on s'offre un miroir.
>
> Gérard Genette

ABSTRACT. At the very core of the pastoral genre is the assumption that its characters are not what they pretend to be. Shepherds and shepherdesses are noble people who have chosen a more tranquil life in order to dedicate themselves to the labors of love. Although they live in a place remote in space or time, their preoccupation and the code of behavior they follow correspond exactly to the ones of the ideal reader or spectator for which the work is intended. This paper exposes the paradox of the shepherd character in the late 1500, and early 1600, in Europe and discusses the pertinence of using the notion of baroque to understand the figure of the shepherd and the pastoral world that surrounds him.

"Pourquoi toujours des bergers? On ne voit que cela partout," declares M. Jourdan to his music teacher in the *Bourgeois Gentilhomme*. Molière in 1670 points to the ubiquitous figure present in all the court festivals of Louis XIV. The music teacher explains that, for reasons of verisimilitude, the shepherds are the characters that are more likely to speak in songs. Is it not a paradox, then, that the objectively less credible characters, these fakes, noble sheep-keepers dressed like princes and endowed with all the most refined social qualities, serve this purpose of verisimilitude? For the France of the second half of the seventeenth century, the notion of verisimilitude rules over every artistic production.

The shepherd has a most ambiguous identity. Although he lives in the countryside and is represented with specific attributes—the crook, the shoulder bag and the hat with wide edges to protect him from the

Going for Baroque: Cultural Transformations1550-1650.
A St. Michael's College Symposium. Francesco Guardiani ed. Ottawa: Legas, 1999

harsh rays of the afternoon sun—it is still somehow a given that he is of aristocratic blood. The crook is made of gold, the bag and costume are made of rich fabrics in elaborate designs. The language he speaks is refined and subtle; his main occupation far from the flock, is to dedicate himself entirely to the requirements of Love.

He is the heir of Theocritus' idealized characters and of Virgil's Meloebius. Unlike them, however, the seventeenth-century shepherd, as he appears in novels and as he invades the French stage[1] lives in a countryside that has no more plausible links with reality. Whereas the antique shepherds live in a pastoral world where winter follows summer, pleasure is interrupted by loss, where the fruits of the earth are harvested with pain and labor, in brief, a world that we might understand as closer to the real country life, the modern shepherd wanders in a fantasyland deprived of any tensions.

This is how pastoral is presented to a relatively wide French readership in 1607 in Honoré d'Urfé's novel *L'Astrée*. It will contribute deeply to the constitution of both the literature of French classicism, and, through the pastoral drama, to the formation of French tragedy.

French pastoral drama is a play, tragi-comic in genre, lyrical in tone, situated in a fabricated locus, a mythical Arcadia or some equivalent. In a fine but dated study of pastoral, Jules Marsan points out the poetical and lyrical qualities of the genre and insists on its position "hors du réel" or even "hors du possible."[2] In this frame, the shepherd, with its ambiguous nature, is even more intriguing. I would like to suggest in this paper, that the shepherd, as he passes on stage, for a short but significant period of time, at the end of the sixteenth and the beginning of the seventeenth century in France, embodies in an unexpected way, some of the most convincing features of the period that we now agree to call "baroque."

---

[1] Between 1561 and 1654, more than 110 pastoral pieces have been numbered in France.

[2] For Jules Marsan, the pastoral drama is "une œuvre dramatique et poétique tout ensemble—poétique au sens large du mot, dans le fond et dans la forme, et non pas seulement oratoire, mais lyrique,—à égale distance de la tragédie et de la comédie, hors du réel, hors du possible parfois, ayant pour objet la peinture de l'amour absolu..." *La pastorale dramatique en France*, 174.

I Historiography of the "baroque littéraire"

We had the opportunity in this symposium to hear interesting discussions from specialists in many fields. Most of them did not seem ill at ease using the terms "baroque" or "neobaroque." When I heard the symposium's title, however, I could not help asking myself why we should "go for baroque"... again? As I was preparing this paper, I remembered the first sentence of Didier Souiller's 1988 book on baroque European literature: "Encore un livre sur le baroque!" "Encore" is the operative word here, and as we foray into this period with this label, we should do so with caution and hear the lesson of our predecessors. By "going for baroque" are we taken again by our own contemporary baroque frenzy, our post World War II quest for a baroque style or baroque themes, as we study late sixteenth and early seventeenth century literature? Or, do we assume that an historical and irresistible impulsion drove the artists of the past to a certain esthetic, a movement, an *épistémé*, that can be analyzed and understood in historical, sociological an ideological terms? Even though my contribution to this symposium will weigh on the second question by investigating the baroque nature of the shepherd, I believe it would be useful to address the former briefly, reviewing the concept of "baroque littéraire" through the particularities of French historiography.

The idea of the baroque itself has been long in the making and frequently contested. As we have learned from Evonne Levey's paper, even for the formalist art historian Heinrich Wölfflin who first tried to identify esthetical categories for the identification of the style, baroque was still a blurred notion. Only in France is the debate so arduous that one feels discouraged from trying to sort things out. One major discomfort comes from the fact that the very notion of artistic baroque in France is not as convincing as it is for Germany, Italy or Spain. It is through classicism that French art achieves its status in the seventeenth century. Still in reaction against the myopia for classicism, Jean Rousset's early 1950s rediscovery of recurrent baroque themes in seventeenth-century literature was received with enthusiasm. His seminal *Littérature de l'âge baroque* (Paris, 1954) has the merit of having rehabilitated forgotten poets and neglected playwrights who devoted themselves to instability, mobility, metamorphosis and ornament. Not for the first time, but in an influential way, the word about the baroque was spread. Its fortune in the French critical discourse of the following decade was such that a synthetic re-evaluation was sorely needed at the end of the 1960s.

Pierre Charpentrat's 1967 cautionary *Mirage baroque*, seems as pertinent today, perhaps more so, as the approaching millenium exacerbates our imaginations. Under the term "baroque," Charpentrat distinguishes five somehow contradictory conceptions. The first one is Jean Rousset's, where baroque is mainly associated with intellectual distance and artificiality, a conception that lead Gérard Genette to think the baroque in poetical terms seeing in it a rare example of a Poetic founded on a Rhetoric. The second conception, and the more widely embraced, is Eugenio d'Ors' vision of a universal baroque that is in fact the Dionysiac side of culture, where liberty and ingenuity is not restrain by any classicism. The third approach is the one of the scholars who are looking for a characteristic baroque style instead of themes. Marcel Raymond's 1949 article in the *Revue des sciences humaines*, is the point of departure of the systematic application of Wölfflin's categories to the literary field: pictorial presentation, view into depth, open form, complex unity, relative clarity. The fourth conception, the more harmful according to Charpentrat, uses the term "baroque" to characterize all the artistic production of a specific period, reducing and flattening its objects. The last definition is given by the dictionaries, the Littré, for instance, where "baroque" is synonymous with bad excess and disorder.

Charpentrat's remarks lead a pioneer like Jean Rousset to rethink the pertinence of a notion that could mean everything and its contrary. A significant chapter entitled "Adieu au baroque" can be found in his 1968 *L'Intérieur et l'extérieur. Essais sur la poésie et sur le théâtre au XVIIe siècle*. There he claims that one can work on seventeenth-century French without bothering about the baroque anymore on the condition that one has assimilated all its particulars[3]. For the late Rousset, baroque remains a tool to question reality.

Charpentrat's 1967 "sottisier"[4] as Rousset calls it, did not put an end to the debate surrounding the baroque. Many "Journées Internationales sur le Baroque" in Montauban kept scholars busy. Despite the

[3] "On peut désormais travailler sur le XVIIe siècle sans plus se soucier du Baroque, à condition d'en avoir assimilé toutes les données." *L'Intérieur et l'extérieur*, 243.

[4] A "sottisier" is a collection of foolish quotations.

controversies, the great interest of the "discovery" of the "baroque littéraire" is that it permitted to reveal a forgotten dix-septième siècle, a non-classical one.

Certain scholars still did not doubt of the pertinence of applying the formal categories identified by the art historians to define a baroque literary character. In the introduction of his *Essai sur l'esprit du héros baroque* (1973), Jean Maillard's is convinced that with a simple "jeu de correspondance,"[5] one can deduce the characteristics of a "baroque hero." The term "jeu" here reveals a tendency of some literary critics to push hermeneutics toward free metaphorical association. Maillard's game, though, is serious, since it leads him to believe in the "parfaite coïcidence" (exact match) between "the baroque hero and the church, the palaces, the costumes and the *fêtes* that surround him."[6] This is where the shoe pinches. If there is rapport between all the arts, it is surely not in terms of "exact match" between all these tropes.

As some were looking for equivalences, other were refining their perspective. Gisèle Mathieu-Castellani, for instance, after unveiling the baroque Eros of French poetry (cf. *Eros Baroque*, and *Mythes de l'Éros baroque*) distinguished between a baroque poetry which goal is to persuade through the intellect and the senses and deliver a message of truth; and a mannerist poetry where the artifice maintains doubts and incredulity, where seduction more than persuasion is involved.[7]

At the end of the 1980s, two books reinterpreted the baroque in French terms. In 1988, Didier Souiller published his *Littérature baroque en Europe* in which he explores the baroque *épistémé* in Europe as a whole and finds a "collective consciousness in baroque Europe" (15), a shared perception of existence as a spectacle of illusory and

[5] A transfer of a set of concepts from the plastic arts—implicitly Wölfflin's categories, mediated by Marcel Raymond—to literature.

[6] "Dès lors que se trouvent, fût-ce sommairement, rappelées les lois générales de cette esthétique, on pourra par un jeu de correspondances en déduire les grands thèmes par quoi le héros baroque révèle tour à tour un comportement et une vision du monde, celle de l'homme des XVIe et XVIIe siècles. On constatera ainsi la parfaite coïncidence entre le héros baroque et l'église baroque qu'il hante, le palais baroque qu'il habite, le costume qu'il porte, les fêtes sur l'eau, les feux d'artifice auxquels il participe." Jean-François Maillard, 20.

[7] This distinction is clearly summarize in the introduction of her anthology, *La Poésie amoureuse de l'âge baroque*.

changing appearances. This perspective escapes the pitfalls of the formalist approach to baroque and its blind application of concepts or categories developed for the visual arts. By looking at what is behind these categories, one can find the source of every manifestations of baroque. Bernard Chedozeau's *Le Baroque*, published a year later, with insightful remarks on the history of religious ideas, focuses on France, even though, he admits the "paradox of defining a baroque literary field in a country that hardly knows artistic baroque" (21). His approach is different from Souiller's. Chédozeau sees that despite the controversies in French baroque historiography, everybody seems to agree on one point. The genres that are called "baroque" or where the characteristics that are identified as baroque are found in theatre, religious eloquence, and epic, heroic or lyric poetry.[8] Chédozeau goes on to map the works that fall outside of the baroque's range—printed texts of intellectual prose. These texts, he argues, are contrary to the baroque and conceived exclusively for the press. They lack an aural component, that is, for Chédozeau, the basis of the "baroque littéraire." As those present at Francesco Guardiani's talk yesterday afternoon can observe, this idea is very close Marshall McLuhan's on that matter. I am not aware that Chédozeau had read the *Gutenberg Galaxy*. In any case, Chédozeau proposes that baroque is in fact a privileged mode of communication, percussive and sensory, that it maintains the quality of oral production (89), and that it implies a total involvement between the writer and the reader, or the actor and the spectator. When this aural component is progressively lost as the production of printed text spreads forth, bringing its own system of beliefs, the baroque retires to the back of the stage.

II The Shepherd as Baroque Character

From this rapid and necessarily incomplete journey into the French historiography of baroque, what can one say about the nature of the shepherd in late sixteenth and early seventeenth-century French lit-

[8] "L'accord est général pour appeler baroques des textes de théâtre, d'éloquence religieuse, des poèmes épiques ou héroïques ou des poésies lyriques, c'est-à-dire des œuvres qui ont été conçues pour être dites, récitées, chantées ou déclamées, et qui n'ont été imprimées par la suite que pour un certain nombre d'entre elles." Chédozeau, 27.

erature? Two short examples will show how "baroque" he really is. For obvious reasons of time, we will only focus on an excerpt from one love poem by the illustrious François Malherbe, and one scene from a pastoral play whose author was provincial and now largely forgotten. These two texts, contemporary but different in nature and reception, exploit a voyeuristic scene, a *topos* of the pastoral.

The shepherd is known to be a particular kind of spectator, a voyeur. Countless are the scene in *L'Astrée* where characters spy other characters and see and hear what was not intended to be seen or heard. And the process is echoed in the gallant poetry. This act of spying can be associated with the reader's own intrusion into the text and could be a device to make the reader conscious of the process of reading, or the spectator aware of the process of watching a play. This kind of doubling is unanimously identified as a baroque device: the "mise en abyme" echoes the "in dept" disposition, one of Wölfflin's categories of baroque art. In Malherbe's *Chanson*, appearance serves to persuade. The poet addresses an honorable beauty and tries to convince her to cede to his amorous passion. In order to inspire love to her, he imagines a scene where two shepherds are surprised in their close embrace:

> Et peut-être à travers des fougères
> Verrons-nous de bergers à bergères,
> Sein contre sein, et bouche contre bouche,
> Naître et finir quelque douce escarmouche.

The rime fougères/bergères is eloquent. It evokes the association of the shepherd with nature, as well as calling up a hidden, thus, secret, kind of nature. Hidden but revealed by art, the shepherds in their tender embraces are revealed, called up by the poet, painted with words, to make the reluctant women to whom the poem is dedicated, feel the same passion for the poet. Following on this highly sensual strophe, is an observation about the moral of the pastoral world, reminiscent of *Aminta*'s "S'ei piace ei lice":

> C'est chez eux qu'amour est à son aise
> Il y saute, il y danse, il y baise,
> Et foule aux pieds les contraintes serviles,
> De tant de lois qui le gênent aux villes.

The opposition City/County, is explicit, the rime aise/baise (to kiss at ease) is clear enough, almost transparent, and the dancing verse "Il y saute, il y danse, il y baise," whose rhythm is amplified by the anaphora, links a kiss to light actions of dancing. It is a brilliant passage, in one of Malherbe's most famous poem. It shows how a most accomplished poet, esteemed for his work on French language and poetry, known for his rigorous and sometime dry approach to versification, can exploit the possibilities of a simple topos. Chédozeau's model of the reader involvement as a fundamental component of the baroque works perfectly in this idyllic piece. Gisèle Mathieu-Castellani would also agree to relate this piece with the baroque.

The second example also satisfies the condition of reader or spectator involvement and demonstrate the fundamental baroque nature of the dramatic genres as spectacles of illusory and changing appearances. Nicolas de Montreux was official poet to Philippe Emmanuel de Lorraine, duke of Mercoeur in Nantes, Brittany. In the fourth scene of the second act of his pastoral drama, *Arimène* (1596), the eponymous hero recalls the events that surrounded an accidental encounter with the cruel shepherdess that he loves, a spectacle that hypnotizes him until he has to intervene to save the sleeping beauty from a lion that shows up unexpectedly. "O quel plaisir, quel bien delicieux / Ont savouré mes miserables yeux!" These two first verses put the whole scene (a total of 134 verses) under the auspices of the Eye. While he was looking for a lost ox :

> D'un sainct hazard i'entre dans un rocher,
> Là où, bons Dieux! bons Dieux, bons Dieux, i'advise
> Seule en un coing, la trop cruelle Alphise.

There follows the relation of the vision, a very vivid painting indeed, a recollection of another *topos* of love poetry, the sleeping beauty. Again, Jean Rousset would have recognized the images and the rhetorical figures that he associated with baroque esthetics; again, baroque categories like pictorial presentation, view into depth and relative clarity can be identified in this segment, as this pastoral drama has the baroque characteristic of being an "open form" of "complex unity." *Arimène* is a court entertainment, a mix of comedy, mythological interludes, songs and dance where the actors and singers often directly address the spectators. The boundaries between the fictional world and the one of the court are voluntarily blurred.

What is of particular interest in the monologue scene of Arimène, is that the vision of the sleeping beauty produces a very particular effect on the shepherd:

> Ce doux obiect en sa veuë gratieuse,
> Arresta lors & mon ame amoureuse
> [...]
> Mon oeil perdoit sa clarté naturelle,
> En contemplant une chose si belle,
> Il vacilloit en son premier pouvoir,
> Ainsi qu'il faict, alors qu'on luy faict voir
> Tout à un coup la terre sablonneuse
> Couverte alors de neige farineuse,
> Ceste blancheur si vifve l'obscurcist,
> Et sa clarté en la sienne trancist.

The soul is stopped, the eye vacillates while it contemplates this very intense light, the beauty of the woman asleep. In his speech, Arimène, in order to evoke this light, makes a comparison rich with antithesis. The intense beauty is compared to the whiteness of the snow that makes the sand where it falls, by contrast, look dark. Arimène opposes "blancheur," and idea of brightness, to "obscurcist," an idea of darkness; "vifve" that in French can mean bright or alive, with "trancist," dead. Again, this sort of writing is generally recognize as characteristic of baroque literary style. The oppositions are not resolved and the significance goes beyond the words themselves. This non resolution of contradictory perception then leads to a state of altered consciousness. Later in his monologue, the shepherd compares his state of mind to the unconsciousness of the sleeping woman:

> ...elle estoit hors de tout sentiment
> Par le sommeil, & moy semblablement
> Par le playsir qui enyvroit mon ame,
> En regardant une si belle dame...

Is this not a pure baroque moment of contemplation and questioning of the validity of perception? Castellani would call it mannerist, but we are still in the realm of what she also agrees to call the "baroque age." By recalling with words this spectacular moment, Arimène allows the spectator to visualize the moment even more intensely than an actual staging of the scene. For a moment the shepherd becomes the poet, until he finally takes part in the action. In this example, all the positive aspects of the baroque are in play. From a formal point of view, we can identify in them a large number of baroque traits: certain antithetic images like Light and Darkness, and Fire and Water that could please Jean Rousset, literary devices like "mise en abyme." Both texts exemplify the "baroque Eros" of Gisèle Mathieu-Castellani, the baroque perception of existence as a spectacle of illusory and changing appearances of Souiller and Chédozeau's conception of a baroque participation of the reader or the spectator through the powers of speech. It is almost too good to be true, as one could easily read the pastoral as nothing less then the prototype of a "baroque littéraire".

Souiller and Chédozeau do not talk about pastoral drama, thus they seem to miss a genre that exemplifies remarkably both their views of the baroque. Both acknowledge the centrality of theatre in this period. Souiller's major field is the picaresque novel, and he mentions the pastoral novel in a chapter entitled "forms of wanderings and pursuits." Chédozeau, on the other hand, sees baroque traits in the novel (among them, *L'Astrée*), exemplifying his hypothesis that the French seventeenth-century novel, although a printed genre, still has some characteristics of the aural tradition. Neither of them, however, addresses the pastoral drama directly.[9]

Along with the aural component of any baroque literature that was stressed by Chedozeau, the figure of the shepherd serves another vision of the baroque, closer to the interpretation of Eugenio d'Ors. Unlike the constricted regulation of dramatic form, character development, and speech characteristic of the classical, the pastoral mode is the locus for the free play of the imagination. What seems to have attract so many writers to the pastoral genre is the exceptional liberty it allowed them. Alexandre Hardy, one of the most prolific French playwright of the beginning of the seventeenth century, gives, in the preface to the third volume of his plays, what he thinks are the qualities of a good "poeme bocager, apellé vulgairement pastorale." He

[9] It might be implicit in Souiller's category of "drame baroque" that includes the English problem play, the French "tragi-comédie" and the Spanish "comedia."

insist on the originality of invention, blaming those who are bluntly copying or translating, and the quality of verses which are neither "prose rimée" nor "rime prosée."[10] Pastoral drama escapes the rigidity of the Aristotelian division of theatre in tragedy and comedy. Its intermediate position even allows a re-evaluation of language itself, half way between prose and verse.

It is, I believe, important to see what writers actually write when they are allowed relative liberty of creation. And this is where, I strongly believe, that the baroque, shall it exists, would be more perceptible.

The shepherds are still present in the literary world after what is considered to be the end of the baroque age in France around 1650. On the stage in the second half of the seventeenth century, at the apex of French classicism, shepherd and shepherdesses fill all the possible spaces that classicism fails to or has not yet conquered. There they assume their intermediary function, linking the acts of a comedy, assuring that the "tragédie lyrique"—the French answer to Italian opera—does not become too tragic, and inviting the court itself to participate in a final "Grand ballet." With this baroque survival in the middle of what posterity traditionally considers like the pinnacle of French classicism, one can speak, like Roland Barthes of "tenebroso racinien," or like Philippe Sellier, of the "rays" and "shadows" of the period following the 1650s. Even if the shepherds become somehow shallower and are reduced to simple types in the second half of the century, their persistently presence serves as a vehicle for a more fantasist mode of artistic expression.

So, is the late sixteenth and early seventeenth-century shepherd some kind of typical or archetypal baroque hero? Characterized by his costume, his environment (the Arcadian landscape), and his preoccupation (love), the shepherd can be just any type. He can be as noble, faithful of unfaithful as you want him to be, he can be as classic or as baroque as you like. In the baroque period, the shepherd plays his role with ease, but he does so from the origins of the pastoral mode, and one would probably find neobaroque traits in his twentieth-century heirs. After all, as Mircea Eliade has stated, the nostalgia for a Golden Age, is one of the last surviving myths of Western civilization. It has

[10] Alexandre Hardy, *Théâtre* III, 1626. The pastoral drama that concludes the volume, *Corinne ou le Silence*, was probably written around 1614.

been said that, as far as the literary field is concerned, the baroque characteristics are most visible in the off-centered genres.[11] In his fabricated world, the shepherd acts as a perfect revealers of the preoccupations of its time.

WORKS CITED

Barthes, Roland. *Sur Racine*. Paris: Seuil, 1963.

Charpentrat, Pierre. *Le mirage baroquue.* Paris: Éditions de Minuit, 1967.

Chédozeau, Bernard. *Le Baroque*. Paris: Nathan, 1989.

D'Ors, Eugenio. *Lo Barroco.* Madrid: Aguilar, 1944.

D'Urfé, Honoré, *L'Astrée*. Trans. Steven Rendall. Binghamton, N.Y. : Medieval & Renaissance Texts & Binghamton, N.Y. : Medieval & Renaissance Texts & Studies, 1995.

Delmas, Christian. Introduction. Corneille, Pierre. *Andromède*. Paris: Nizet, 1974.

Hardy, Alexandre. *Théâtre*. Paris: Quesnel, 1626.

Maillard, Jean-François. *Essai sur l'esprit du héros baroque 1580-1640. Le même et l'autre*. Paris: Nizet, 1973.

Marsan, Jules. *La pastorale dramatique en France* (Paris, 1905). Geneva: Slatkine, 1969.

Mathieu-Castellani, Gisèle ed.. *La Poésie amoureuse de l'âge baroque*. Paris: Livre de Poche, 1990.

Mathieu-Castellani, Gisèle. *Eros Baroque*. Paris: U.G.E., 1979.

__________. *Mythes de l'Éros baroque*, Paris, PUF, 1981.

Montreux, Nicholas de, *L'Arimène*. Nantes: Doriou, 1597.

Rousset, Jean. *L'Intérieur et l'extérieur*. Paris: Corti, 1968.

__________. *La littérature de l'âge baroque.* Paris: Corti, 1954.

Sellier, Philippe. "Les rayons et les ombres." *Et in Arcadia ego.* Ed. Antoine Soare. Paris-Seattle-Tübingen: Biblio 17, 1997. 301-314.

Souiller, Didier. *La littérature baroque en Europe*. Paris: PUF, 1988.

[11] Christian Delmas, introduction of Pierre Corneille's *Andromède*, "C'est dans les genres les moins littéraires, ballets et tragi-comédies, ou dans les à-côtés de la littérature, mise en scène et décoration que se reconnaissent le plus aisément les thèmes baroques" (XVI).

Anna Migliarisi

Directing Opera in the Italian Baroque

ABSTRACT. *Il Corago* (1628) is an anonymous treatise by a professional director of the early baroque theatre, discovered in 1975 and published for the first time in 1983. It deals with virtually every aspect of directing both musical and spoken drama, from selecting the play-text and directing actors and choral ensembles to matters of scenography and the organisation of the performance. In this paper I will discuss the author's conception of the unifying role of the corago in Baroque opera, which he describes as a hybrid of "ten or twelve arts," including poetry, music, dance, painting, and architecture.

One of the defining features of the art we call baroque is a complete impression of unity of the arts on a grand scale. Opera, which embraces such arts as poetry, vocal and instrumental music, scenery, costumes, acting and dancing, is a perfect reflection of this. Naturally such a complex theatrical form requires the presence of a forceful director to synthesize its constituent parts into a unified aesthetic vision. However, as Roger Savage observes, "...one sometimes hears that the staging of opera before 1900 is ... a closed and irrelevant book to us, that anyway it was always a ramshackle and inadequate affair" (363-4). And most historians of the theatre claim the advent of naturalism and the new dramas of realism brought the modern director into being. In their introduction to *Directors on Directing*, a standard source book on the art of direction, Toby Cole and Helen Krich Chinoy claim that, before the end of the nineteenth century, "the director did not even have a name, for the terms 'director', *regisseur* and *metter en scene* had barely begun to acquire their present meaning" (3).

The general assumption of most theatre historians is that prior to the 1850s or so the director is a shadowy, underdeveloped figure rather than a professional functionary. The Duke of Saxe-Meiningen (1826-1914) is generally cited as the first modern regisseur (Brockett 429).

Going for Baroque: Cultural Transformations1550-1650.
A St. Michael's College Symposium. Francesco Guardiani ed. Ottawa: Legas, 1999

Impromptu at Versailles and *Hamlet* are cited as seminal but embryonic considerations of the director's craft. Both Moliere and Shakespeare figure prominently as director-authors but with the emphasis on their activities as authors, while the medieval stage manager is usually regarded as no more than a precursor of the director. In fact, according to standard theatre sources, there were no directors, in the full sense of the term, till the end of the nineteenth century. In what follows, I will discuss a treatise on the art of directing written in 1628—one of several treatises on directing written in late Renaissance and early Baroque Italy—that calls into question this common view.

Il Corago o vero alcune osservazioni per mettere ben in scena le composizioni drammatiche (c. 1628) is an anonymous treatise by a director of the early baroque theatre, discovered in 1975 and published for the first time in only 1983. Except for a few pages in English translation, this edition, by Paolo Fabbri and Angelo Pompilio, is the only one,in existence, a fact that fully explains why a work of this calibre has received virtually no attention by theatre historians (although a handful of musicologists have recognized its significance in the context of the staging of early opera, or, as it was also called, princely or courtly opera).[1] In their introduction, Fabbri and Pompilio suggest that the treatise was written by Pierfrancesco Rinuccini, son of the renowned poet Ottavio Rinuccini of Florence, but they are obviously not convinced of this since they have published the work as anonymous.[2]

The word *corago* is the author's term for director. In classical Greece the term *choregos* described the individual who financed and

[1] By early opera I mean musical drama produced between 1590 and the opening of the first public opera house, the Teatro San Cassiano in Venice, in 1637.

[2] This edition is far from perfect since the editors were unable to decipher various passages in the manuscript, including: "torcie agude [?]",39; "Nucciano [= Facciamo?], di cio chiaro [= chiara]" 43; "prima perche pare moralmente [?]" 57; "partorisce inesti [?] pi[u] belli" 81; "molto piu viva [=vivo] e quasi arieggiante [?] e l'istromento di corde" 85; "prourera per quanto si mostrera possibile di imitar li eccellenti cantori ma [mettendo quelli] esangui et in eta nel recitare in part che non siano molto attuosi" 91-2. Extracts in English translation may be found in Roger Savage and Matteo Sansone, (495-511).

coordinated theatrical performances; in classical Rome the *choragus* sometimes extended his function to include the choreography of the chorus[3]. According to the author of our treatise, both the term and the art of the ancient *corago*, as a "vital support for dramatic poetry" were lost in modern times:

> ...così quelle arti che a ciò particolarmente servivano si sono o affatto o in gran parte perdute. Tra queste l'arte del corago antico, necessario sussidio della poesia drammatica, e di modo spente che o noi [= non] ha piu neanche nome propio appresso l'italiani o, se ritiene quel antico, egli e communemente ignoto alla maggior parte[4].

Although the term *corago* was lost, the art itself was actually not lost, since we had a number of professional directors in late Renaissance and early Baroque Italy, including, Leone De Sommi, Angelo Ingegneri, Emilio De' Cavalieri, Marco Da Gagliano, the directors of the *commedia dell'arte*, and others.[5] Clearly, the author of *Il Corago* sees this art in a different perspective because, unlike his predecessors, he focuses on musical drama as well as spoken drama.

---

[3] For further discussion see Walton, *Greek Theatre Practice;* Duckworth, *The Nature of Roman Comedy: A Study in Popular Entertainment*; and Arnott, *The Ancient Greek and Roman Theatre.* In modern Italian the Greek term is translated *corego.*

[4] "...the art of the ancient corago, as a vital support for dramatic poetry, is so obliterated that to Italians it no longer even has a name of its own, or if it does keep the old one, most people do not know what it means." *Il corago* 21.

[5] Emilio De' Cavalieri (1550-1602) was a composer as well as the director of musical activities at the Medici court in Florence in the 1580s. In 1600 his sacred opera *Rappresentazione de Anima, et di Corpo* was produced in Rome. In the *Preface* to this work, Cavalieri provides instructions to the director wishing to perform "this present work or others like it." Marco Da Gagliano (1575-1642), considered to be one of the most prolific composers of the period, served as a director of musical theatre in Florence in the early 1600's. In 1608 he directed his opera *Dafne* at the Court of Mantua. In the *Preface* to this work, Da Gagliano provides a thorough account of the production from a directorial point of view (Marco Da Gagliano in MacClintock). Directors of the *commedia dell'arte* include Pier Maria Cecchini, Virginia Ramponi, Vittoria Piissimi and Diane De Ponti. See K. and L. Richards *The Commedia dell'arte.*

The author's purpose in writing this treatise is to define the art of the modern *corago* in all of its parts. The treatise is divided into twenty-three chapters, the first of which is devoted to an explication of the role and function of the director in theatrical representation, which he defines as a hybrid of ten or twelve arts including poetry, music, dance, painting and architecture.

This discussion is followed by instructions to the director (of both musical and spoken drama) on scenography, dramatic and musical composition, directing actors and choral ensembles, dance and combat choreography, designing costumes, the use of stage machinery, stage illumination, and the organization of performance. The instructions are detailed, highly technical (in his notes to the composer, for example, he deals with metrics, scales, melodic arrangements, and so on), and they are typically prefaced by a comparison between modern and ancient practice.

One of the distinguishing features of *Il corago*, compared to the treatises of his predecessors such as De Sommi and Ingegneri, is the scope of the author's instructions. He deals with virtually every aspect of directorial theory and practice, and with the staging problems peculiar to each theatrical genre (with the exception of improvised theatre). The author pays considerable attention to the treatment of *balli*, promenades, simulated stage-battles, the integration of music in performance, and the creation of special effects with modern stage machines, which, by the middle of the seventeenth century, was a requisite feature of Baroque production. The author devotes eight of the twenty-three chapters to musical drama, which suggests that by the time *Il corago* was written, about 1628, opera had achieved sufficient recognition as an autonomous theatrical genre to warrant an independent detailed treatment from a directorial point of view.

I will now describe the author's conception of the role and function of the *corago* (and of his strategic position in the hierarchy of theatrical representation), and then focus in on three aspects of his instructions - working with actors, using stage machines, and organizing production. My purpose is to illustrate that the theory and methodology prescribed in this treatise is not significantly different than what constitutes modern directorial practice.

In chapter one of *Il corago*, the author defines the art of the modern *corago* as that faculty or competence ["quello facolta mendiante"] that enables an individual, utilizing the available means and methods, to transform the poetic text into a staged performance with the perfection it requires. The end of theatrical representation, the author maintains, is to arouse admiration and delight in the spectator in order to instill a fruitful moral utility.[6] This definition reflects the author's humanist preoccupation with emulating classical excellence in modern productions, and in particular musical drama. However, as subsequent chapters of the treatise make clear, this view overlaps with the aesthetic premises of the Baroque period - the intense expression of the text (literary or musical) by the grand *maniera*, the focus of the entertainment on the `spectacular' and *effetti meravigliosi*, the `marvellous', as symbols of the ability of the moderns to surpass the ancients[7].

In the view of the author, the director is the servant of the poem, that is to say, the performance on the stage must be coincident with the meaning and feeling which the author wishes to convey as set down in the literary text. In order to achieve this end, the *corago* requires the assistance of the following arts. One, the arts of carpentry and masonry to oversee the design and construction of the stage. Two, the art of architecture for the design of the scenic houses, palaces, temples and the like. Three, the art of perspective painting for the scenery and perspective vistas. Four, the art of dressmakers and tailors to provide the performers with beautifully designed costumes. Five, the art of acting in order to instruct and guide the actors in the scenic action. Six, the art of music, whether instrumental or vocal. Seven, the art of dance for the choreography of *balli*, processions and choral formations. Eight, the arts of combat and fencing for tourneys and scenes of warfare. Nine, the art of mechanics for the display of marvellous effects on land, sea and in the heavens. And, ten, the art of lighting for basic illumination as well as the creation of special effects (*Il corago* 22).

By way of this extensive definition, the author concludes that the *corago* must have a general knowledge of these various arts in order

[6] "noi per l'arte del corago intenderemo qui quello facolta mendiante la quale l'uomo sa prescrivere tutti quie mezzi e modi che sono necassarii accio che una azione drammatica gia composta dal poeta sia portata in scena con la perfezione che si richiede per insinuare con ammirazione e diletto quella utilita e frutto anche morale che la poesia rechiedera. *Il corago* 21.

[7] For discussion see Maniates, *Mannerism in Italian Music and Culture*.

that he may guide and exercise command over the designers, machinists, painters, architects, actors, in short, all of the collaborative artists throughout the production. However, the author maintains that it is essential that the director be accomplished in the arts of the actor and the machinist, on the grounds that these are the arts that he will call upon most frequently in modern productions.[8]

Our author views representation, whether comedy, tragedy, pastoral or the sung drama, as an art form with its own values, a composite of disparate elements, "dieci o dodici arti" ten or twelve arts (*Il corago* 23), each with its own guiding principles and language. It is the task of the director to gain proficiency in each of these languages in order to facilitate the discourse of performance.

The author observes that each of these ten or twelve independent arts is sufficient in itself to create pleasure and delight ["diletto e meraviglia grandissima"] in the spectator viewing the performance. A well-written tragedy arouses pleasure simply in the reading. Listening to and watching an actor on the stage performing his role with noble presence, good voice, graceful beauty and manners, provokes applause. Beautifully designed and constructed costumes, handsome stage architecture, excellent singing, and a display of scenic marvels arouse the passionate curiosity ["impetua curiosita"] of the spectator. If the impact of each of these arts on its own is enough to captivate the spectator, then "una opera mesta [= mista]", that is, a composite of all these artifices in a theatrical performance, creates a heightened overall impression which affectively moves the spectator (Il corago 23).

Working with actors

In his instructions on working with actors, our author distinguishes between spoken and sung drama but maintains that the art of acting is based on a foundation of sound principles that apply to all modes of performance.

[8] In chapter twenty-one, "delle machine", the author claims that modern stage machinery is the most persuasive means of producing intense, immediate emotional responses in the spectator. *Il corago* 116.

Our author maintains that in order to be a good musical theatre performer one must be, above all, a good speaking actor, and he strongly urges the director of the sung drama to cast a good actor over an excellent singer with little or no talent for acting.[9] Like his contemporaries, the author holds the work of the actor in high regard and observes that while some connoisseurs of music appreciate excellent singers, however cold their acting ["quantunque freddi nel recitamento"], the common spectator derives most satisfaction from watching highly skilled actors ["perfetti istrioni"] with mediocre vocal and musical skills (*Il corago* 91).

In order to facilitate excellence in performance, the *corago* must be familiar with the fundamentals of voice production, the mechanics of speech, stage movement, delivery, memory and the psychology of humours. He must also possess a method of working with individual actors as well as choral ensembles and supernumeraries.

Throughout the treatise, our author refers to the director as the instructor and guide of the actors, a conception not significantly different from that of Moliere in his *Impromptu at Versailles* (1663). As the figure with the strategic view of the whole, it is the task of the director to observe, assess and guide critically throughout the rehearsal process, in order to ensure that, in performance, the actor contributes to the revelation of character, situation, meaning and feeling with an effective delivery.

Naturally this dominant position imposes a tremendous responsibility on the director, who requires a thorough command of the actor's art as well as sound judgment in order to facilitate excellence in the performer. According to our author, the naturally gifted actor can be stifled and in some cases `ruined' by poor instruction from the director[10].

This potential peril is to a certain extent a function of the actor-director relationship itself, which is the only transaction in theatrical

[9] "Sopra tutto per esser buon recitante cantando bisognerebbe esser anche buono recitante parlando, onde aviamo veduto che alcuni che hanno avuto particolare grazia in recitare hanno fatto meraviglia quando insieme hanno saputo cantare." *Il corago* 91.

[10] "...credo sia non solo dalla naturalezza che a cio si richiede avere, ma ancora da non ritrovarsi chi sappia loro insegnare il modo di ben recitare.." *Il corago* 96.

production which proceeds without an intermediary (such as the paint and canvas of the scenic designer, the textiles of the costume designer, and so on). The actor's raw materials are his body, his voice and his emotions, a fact which suggests that "good instructions" are the fruit of a cultivated sensibility on the part of the director as well as a certain attitude towards the work. In modern theatrical practice this is the essence of professionalism.

Stage machinery

As for the art of the stage machinist, our author maintains that the director must be trained in the design, the construction, and the method of operation of various stage machines, finding ways to raise, lower and make vanish clouds, sea monsters, celestial deities, infernal creatures and the like on land, sea and in the heavens because they are the most persuasive means of producing intense, immediate, emotional responses in the modern spectator ["rapischino gli animi delli spettatori"], who delights in witnessing supernatural phenomena that trick the eye and the senses (*Il corago* 116).

In this section the author itemizes what he considers to be the representative scenic effects which the modern director may make use of in production, and he refers the reader to a series of plates illustrating the machines whereby these effects can be produced. These plates are not extant; however, they include: celestial deities descending from the heavens to the earth in radiant clouds; celestial choirs and assemblies suspended in the heavens; Furies and other infernal creatures rising from the depths of the earth and flying in mid-air; fantastical creatures such as giants, ghosts and seven-headed monsters who sprout seven heads when one is cut off; scenic tempests with lightning, thunder and hail; earthquakes and tremors; crumbling city walls for military scenes; and marine scenes depicting billowy waves with moving ships, sirens and other exotic creatures of the deep (*Il corago* 116-23).

In this chapter the author also instructs the director in various ways of raising and lowering the front curtain, in methods of scene-changing, which always occurred in full view of the spectator, and in the treatment of the stage heavens - the ceiling of the theatre - and the stage floor, which housed wondrous machines that would make sudden appearances through trap-doors.

The author's principal concerns in this discussion are that the director makes use of the entire stage picture (ceiling, wings, orchestra), taking into account advances in scenography and stage machinery, and that the transformations in scenery, the entrances of the machines and the shifts in lighting occur simultaneously—the total effect is key—in order to create magical effects that illicit gasps of surprise in the spectator and leave him virtually breathless by the splendour of the *mise en scene* - which constitutes a central aesthetic premise of Baroque production. Excellence could be measured by the extent to which the "illusion", which was always contrived, always rhetorical, could illicit an intense emotional response from the spectator.

The *mise en scene* of classicism, which was essentially illustrative and characterized by balance, economy, a central vanishing-point, and a sense of reality that was "contained", gives way, in Baroque production, to movement, transformation, a play with real and fictive space and *effetti meravigliosi*, marvellous effects, which strain the boundaries of verisimilitude and which actively engage the spectator in the spatial-psychological field created.

Organization of the performance

The *opera mista* is a composite art form which depends on the synthesis of diverse talents both on and off the stage. Before the final performance begins, the director "completes" his function by ensuring that both the cast and crew are properly assembled and prepared to play their parts. The author concludes his treatise with a checklist intended to assist the director with the organization of the final performance, in which he functions as a super stage manager.

I wish to draw attention to the fact that the *corago*, as described by our author, appears to have his hands in virtually every aspect of early Baroque production - from assessing the merits of the literary text, working with the composer and librettist, supervising the work of painters and architects, and working with the actors and singers to the organization of the final performance - in short, all of the arts converge with the *corago*.

The director is advised to see to it that all of the actors are situated backstage at their respective entrances fully dressed in their costumes and prepared to enter the scene as required. The crew assigned to operate the stage machinery must be located at their respective stations, not leaving them without the permission of the director. Tailors and dressers must be located at the appropriate entrances of the playing area to assist the performers with quick changes of costumes (*Il corago* 125).

The musicians must have their instruments tuned before the curtain goes up because, according to the author, it is unpleasant to hear an instrument being tuned once the action on the stage has begun. The director must ensure that the machines have been well oiled or soaped to prevent distracting noises as they ascend or descend. The author observes that it is annoying to witness a technician enter the scene in order to adjust the machinery during the performance, and he cites an incident at the 1628 performance at Parma where this occurred (*Il corago* 125).

The director must check in advance all the ropes and pulleys of the machines:

> perche si trova alle volte alcuni tanto maligni che senza rispetto alcuno del prinipe e per malignita o invidia che portono al corago o architetto tagliano le corde o altrementi guastano quelli ordigni accio le macchine non si possino alzare o rovinino.[11]

The author maintains that he has himself witnessed this outright sabotage in performances held in Florence. To prevent such occurrences, the director is advised to assign trustworthy technicians to supervise the operation of each machine[12].

[11] "there are sometimes malicious people who, without any respect for the prince and out of malice and envy for the director or the architect, cut or damage the ropes and pulleys so that the machines cannot be raised or they crash down." *Il corago* 125.

[12] The author does not specify either the performance or the malfunctioning machine. Savage and Sansone suggest it was the machine in *Mercurio e Marte*, which raised three Furies from below the stage and which the author refers to as "dangerous" in chapter twenty-one. For further discussion see Savage and Sansone 510, footnote 52. Outright sabotage seems to have been a common concern for directors in the theatre throughout this period. In

With respect to the movements of the actors and crew backstage, the author maintains that it is essential that performers and personnel alike avoid leaning out of the perspectives at any time during the performance to gaze out into the auditorium. This inappropriate conduct is not only visually displeasing but it may hinder the movements of the *periaktoi* and stage machinery. The author acknowledges that this may be a very difficult rule to enforce and observes that the Grand Duke Cosimo was only able to prevent this conduct by keeping two dwarfs backstage who would shoot with crossbows at anyone leaning out[13].

Finally, the director must ensure that the lighting crew is stationed at their respective positions behind the perspectives and in the wings, again assigning this area of production to trustworthy individuals who do nothing but control the lights, keeping them alight and remedying any fault ["ogni male"] which might occur during the performance. By "ogni male" the author is referring to the outbreak of fire in the theatre, which was a common concern through this period, remedied by vessels of water positioned in strategic locales backstage (Sabbattini, in Hewitt 98-99).

These instructions suggest the kind of environment in which musical drama flourished, full of jealousy, intrigue and danger. This is not altogether surprising since early opera, like its predecessor the *intermedio*, was developed and perfected in a courtly context; it was deliberately employed as a diplomatic weapon to impress and outshine competitive courts - a subject which has been well documented by scholars such as Cesare Molinari, Roy Strong, and others.

What is not mentioned in this area of production is the nature of the signal system employed to cue the performers, the musicians and the technicians from behind the perspectives and the wings and under the trap doors on the stage. The checklist provided by the author of *Il*

Pratica de fabricar scene e machine ne' teatri (1638), Nicola Sabbattini recommends that "great care" be taken to designate trustworthy and sincere men to the operation of the machinery and periaktoi (Sabbattini, in Hewitt 105). A humorous treatment of this problem is found in Gian Lorenzo Bernini, *The Impresario*.

[13] Cf. *Il corago* 125. Savage and Sansone maintain that the author is referring to Cosimo II de' Medici who was associated with the productions of *Il giudizio di Paride*,1608, and *Liberazione de Tirreno*,1617 (Savage and Sansone, footnote 56).

corago suggests that the director physically walked from one entrance and piece of technical apparatus to the next to ensure that the actors and crew-members were positioned at their respective entrance or stage machine - a function which in modern theatrical practice is generally assigned to the stage manger and his assistants. However, whether the director remained backstage during the entire performance to cue technicians and literally conduct the movements of the actors or simply retired to a seat in the auditorium once the performance began, cannot be determined.

In conclusion, some of the author's instructions are not entirely original, since both De Sommi and Ingegneri, in their respective treatises, deal with the work of the actor, the analysis of the text, creating a *mise en scene*, and organizing the final performance. With respect to musical drama, the author's contemporary, Da Gagliano, describes the essential features of opera in a manner which is not considerably different than the author's conception. He also provides us with a brief yet highly detailed treatment of a musical-dramatic performance from a directorial point of view in *Preface to Dafne* (1608). However, originality is not necessarily a criterion of excellence; these crosscurrents point to an established tradition in directorial practice, which *Il corago* reflects.

Compared to De Sommi, Ingegneri, and his contemporaries in musical drama, *Il corago* is an important work because it provides us with a comprehensive summary of directorial, as well as musical-dramatic, practice in the late Renaissance and early Baroque periods in Italy. Perhaps the most important aspect of the treatise is that the author formalizes the unifying role of the *corago* in concrete terms, which suggests that by the time *Il corago* was written, directing had achieved a certain recognition as an independent art.

WORKS CITED

Arnott, Peter. *The Ancient Greek and Roman Theatre* 1st ed. New York: Random House, 1971.

Bernini, Gian Lorenzo *The Impresario*. Translation, introduction and notes by Donald Beecher and Massimo Ciavolella. Ottawa: Dovehouse, 1985.

Brockett, Oscar. *History of the Theatre*. Boston: Allyn and Bacon, 1995.

Cole, Toby and Helen Krich Chinoy, eds. *Directors on Directing: A Source Book of the Modern Theatre*, with an illustrated History of Directing by Helen Krich Chnioy, 9th ed. New York: Bobbs-Merrill, 1953.

Corago (Il) o vero alcune osservazioni per mettere ben in scena le composizioni drammatiche. Eds. Paolo Fabbri and Angelo Pompilio. Firenze: Olschki, 1983.

De' Cavalieri, Emilio. *Preface to Rappresentazione de Anima, et di Corpo. Readings in the History of Music in Performance*. Selected, translated and edited by Carol MacClintock. Blomington and London: Indiana UP, 1979.

Duckworth, George. Eckel. *The Nature of Roman Comedy: A Study in Popular Entertainment*. Princeton: Princeton UP, 1952.

Hewitt, Barnard ed. *The Renaissance Stage: Documents of Serlio, Sabbattini and Furtenbach*. Florida: U Miami P, 1958.

MacClintock, Carol. See De' Cavalieri.

Maniates, Maria Rika. *Mannerism in Italian Music and Culture*. Chapel Hill: U of North Carolina P, 1979.

Richards, Kenneth and Laura. *The Commedia dell'arte*. Oxford: Blackwell, 1990.

Savage, Roger and Matteo Sansone. "*Il Corago* and the staging of early opera: four chapters from an anonymous treatise circa 1630." *Early Music* Vol 17.4 (November 1989): 495-511.

Savage, Roger. *The Oxford Illustrated History of Opera.* Oxford and New York: Oxford UP, 1994.

Walton, J. Michael. *Greek Theatre Practice*. Westport: Metheun, 1980.

Laura Willett

Montaigne, Caravaggio and the Conversion of St Paul

ABSTRACT. The conversion of St. Paul, as told in the Acts of the Apostles IX 3-9, is a subject frequently treated by major Renaissance and Baroque painters (Michelangelo, Raphael, Tintoretto, Caravaggio...). It is also used as an unacknowledged model by post-Tridentine writers in a way that underscores the increasing recourse to moral and theatrical criteria in artistic expression. Montaigne is one such writer. Though insisting he has nothing saintly about him, he describes a crucial episode in his life—his fall from a horse and subsequent loss of consciousness—as clearly Pauline experience. My paper will examine the implications of this choice and the artistic function of such a representation.

After the miraculous birth, life, death, and resurrection of Christ, the conversion of Saul of Tarsus into the Apostle Paul was clearly one of the most significant events among those that determined the history of Christianity. It was so important, in fact, that St Luke recounted it no fewer than three times in the *Acts of the Apostles*, a book that is not otherwise noted for its narrative prolixity. The first account, perhaps the most familiar, occurs in Chapter 9, vv. 3-9, and is told in the narrator's third person voice. The second (*Acts* 22, vv. 6-13) purports to be a Greek translation of a version of the event as told in Hebrew by Paul himself, and is thus in the first person; as is the third account (*Acts* 26, vv.12-18), which is also Paul's retelling of the story, but this time in Greek. While not always mutually contradictory, these three accounts are not completely identical either. Each one contains details not found in the other two; put together they establish the full story of the conversion and its purpose.

Taken as a whole, the three accounts add up to this: commissioned by the high priests in Jerusalem to eradicate Christianity in Damascus, Paul set out for the latter city in the company of some other travellers.

Going for Baroque: Cultural Transformations1550-1650.
A St. Michael's College Symposium. Francesco Guardiani ed. Ottawa: Legas, 1999

Just as he was about to reach his destination, at midday, a light from heaven, brighter than the sun itself, suddenly descended around him. The force was such that he fell to the ground blinded, then heard the voice of Christ asking why Paul was persecuting him. Paul's fellow-travellers may or may not have seen the light, may or may not have fallen to the ground, and may or may not have heard the voice (the three versions do not agree on these points). Paul was then ordered by the voice to rise to his feet and continue on to Damascus, into which he was brought by his travelling companions. There he remained three days (this interval is omitted in *Acts* 22), neither eating nor drinking and still in a state of blindness, until the disciple Ananias came to him. Christ's avowed purpose in blinding Paul in this way was to distinguish him from the mass of the people and to make him a witness to what he had seen. From having himself experienced physical blindness and healing, Paul would be able to open the spiritual eyes of the people and bring them from darkness into light.

There is a great deal of debate among Lucan scholars concerning the interpretation of the Greek text and the explanation for the recurring accounts with their apparent factual contradictions (cf. D. M. Stanley, "Paul's Conversion in Acts: Why the Three Accounts?"). In the last decade or two the exegetical trend has been to attribute to Luke's literary design a complex system of clues and reminders, allusions and elements of suspense, developed from one account to another.[1] In other words, the narrator is relying on the reader's ability and desire to play intratextual detective and construct the deeper unity beneath a disjointed surface. For the purposes of our analysis, the essential elements of this miracle story seem to be: the presence of travelling companions, the sudden and all-enveloping nature of the flash of lightning, the fall to the ground, the correlative act of Paul's rising again to his feet, and the pervasive presence of luminosity. It is excessive luminosity—a bright light at midday—that causes Paul's blindness, and luminosity (rather than darkness) that is its principal characteristic. But, paradoxically, luminosity is also the state of enlightenment into which he is to bring the Gentiles. There is no indication

[1] Cf. C.W. Hedrick's "Paul's Conversion-Call: A Comparative Analysis of the Three Reports in Acts," Marvin W. Meyer's "The Light and Voice on the Damascus Road," and D. Hamm's "Paul's Blindness and Its Healing: Clues to Symbolic Intent."

in *Acts* that Paul was proceeding any way but on foot, however, by the end of the twelfth century, iconography was showing him on horseback (Friedlaender 3).

Most likely in the year 1568—the author is deliberately vague as to the date—as Montaigne was riding home from a brief outing, he was knocked to the ground in a violent collision with a powerful draft horse being driven at a gallop by one of his farmhands. In Book II, chap. 6 of the *Essays*, entitled "On Practice," Montaigne describes this collision and its sequel in a way that is strongly reminiscent of the tale of Paul's conversion, recounting the events more than once and even using in places the same language as the *New Testament* text. The shock of the accident is rendered first by "foudroier"/ "strike with thunder" and, in the re-telling, by "esclair"/ "flash of lightning." The first of these derives from *fulgere* via *fulgurare*, both of which are used (in compound forms) to describe in Latin Paul's perception of the sudden blinding light that enveloped him; in the Greek original, compounds of *astrape*, "bolt of lightning," represent the experience.[2] He appears to have suffered some kind of concussion in the fall, and had to be stood on his feet and then carried to his house by his farmhands ("mes gens"/ "my men"), who are transformed in the process of the telling into "those who were with me" (an exact translation of both the Greek and Latin expressions used in *Acts* 22:9). He remained more or less unconscious for two or three hours (the only thing he could really perceive was light, but seemed, like Paul, to hear and see things that those around him of course could not), had what he believed to be the experience of dying, and did not fully recover his senses for about three days. The effect of this experience was to give Montaigne insight into the real nature of death without actually dying, thus enabling him to do that which—as he tells in the opening pages of the chapter—had eluded others before him: to describe what it is

[2] Montaigne's *Essais* are quoted throughout from D. Frame's translation, with reference to the Villey-Saulnier edition of the French original (Paris: Presses Universitaires de France, 1965). For the Greek and Latin New Testaments I have used the following: *Novum Testamentum graece et latine diligentia Des. Erasmi Roterod. Emendatissimum* (Basel: N. Bryling, 1546); *The Interlinear Greek-English New Testament*, trans. Rev. A. Marshall (2nd ed., London: S. Bagster, 1966); *Biblia sacra latina ex biblia sacra vulgatae editionis Sixti V. et Clementis VIII* (London: S. Bagster, [n. d.]); Erasmus, *Paraphrase on the Acts of the Apostles.*

like to die. Like S[t] Paul, Montaigne is thus selected out of the mass in order to teach the rest of humanity the fundamental mystery of human life. Death is often conceived as a passage from light into darkness, but for Montaigne it is the opposite, both in this chapter and elsewhere. Thus another parallel with S[t] Paul, whose vocation—like that of his own prototype, Christ—is to bring the Gentiles from darkness into light.

A commission received by Caravaggio in 1600 to decorate the newly-acquired chapel of Monsignor Cerasi in Santa Maria del Popolo, in Rome, resulted in not one but two depictions of *The Conversion of Saint Paul*. The first of these must in retrospect be considered "practice" or an "essay" of the subject, since it was ultimately rejected by the commissioner and led to a wholly changed and perfected representation. It is the second, more intimate, version which is now universally recognized and admired (Fig. 1). The painter has chosen to represent the very instant where Saul, already knocked to the earth and flooded with the divine presence in the form of intense light, is being transformed into Paul the Apostle. The enormous horse towering above him, whose bit is held by a seemingly oblivious attendant, commands the spectator's attention by its very weight and size, which fills two-thirds of the picture frame, initially obscuring the sense of the scene and the sight of Paul. These three figures, then, or two if we consider that the soldierly Saul and his horse are the essential players, are spotlighted and magnified in such a way that—unlike the settings of Caravaggio's pictorial predecessors—no other figure is visible: they constitute a central group cut off from the rest of the world by the unnaturally tight picture frame.[3] The composition is here simplified almost to abstraction, and isolated for the purpose of examining the psychological dynamics of a purportedly historical event. The spectator is however adduced to read this pictorial narrative in a specific manner and order, and, similarly to both Luke's and Montaigne's story-telling techniques, Caravaggio's own interpretation of the miracle is imposed on us no less by this peculiar presentation. We return to the commonality of these techniques below.

[3] Compare Caravaggio's innovative perspective with those of Raphael and Michelangelo, who are only two among many previous painters who treated this theme (see below). Caravaggio's final version differs from his own earlier one in much the same respect.

Montaigne begins his recollection as in *Acts* 9, as a travel story with the classical motifs of a healing story. But onto these already are grafted certain phrases and events which parallel Luke's triple narrative. "I went riding one day about a league from my house, which is situated at the very hub of all the turmoil of the civil wars in France. Thinking myself perfectly safe, and so near my home…I took a very easy but not very strong horse. On my return…" Likewise, as Saul transits between Jerusalem, the center of religious strife, and Damascus, he is struck down just as he is nearing his destination. A parallel synopsis of the events in *Acts* 9, 22, and 26, alongside Montaigne's account, would reveal that, both lexically and thematically, the similarities are overwhelming. For present purposes, comparison among our three authors will be limited to the essentials. The first rendition of the violent accident, however, merits closer attention:

> On my return, when a sudden occasion came up for me to use this horse for a service to which it was not accustomed, one of my men, big and strong, riding a powerful work horse who had a desperately hard mouth and was moreover fresh and vigorous—this man, in order to show off and get ahead of his companions, spurred his horse at full speed up the path behind me, came down like a colossus on the little man and little horse, and hit us like a thunderbolt with all his strength and weight, sending us both head over heels. So that there lay the horse bowled over and stunned, and me [*moi*] ten or twelve paces beyond, dead, stretched on my back, my face all bruised and skinned, my sword, which I had had in my hand, more than twelve paces away, my belt in pieces, having no more motion or feeling than a log. [emphasis added]

Most remarkable here is the image of the thunderbolt, for it translates in the first place a divine encounter according to the metaphorical tradition of Old Testament theophanies, although the voice of God expressed in the form of thunder also occurs in several places in the New Testament.[4] In the second place, the choice to represent the

[4] Meyer notes that in the context of revelation during theophanies, "voice" is sometimes translated "in thunder," e.g. in *Psalms*, God reveals Himself in thunder and lightning. Within the literature of world religions, "light and voice converge, sometimes as lightning and thunder, in a unified experience of the divine" (33).

shock in terms of *orality* (that is to say, thunder as symbolic of God's voice), rather than light also brings Montaigne's first account into conformity with the version presented in *Acts* 9.[5] Notable too is the subtle transfer effected by an increasingly elliptical style as the author separates and distances himself from the scene in which he is both protagonist, along with the horse, and spectator: "there lay the horse, and me [not "I"]...beyond, dead,...my sword...more than ten paces away, my belt in pieces, etc." He has thus signaled—syntactically and grammatically as well as semantically—an alienation from the body that lies on earth, and he prepares to move into the realm of psychological exploration which will fill the central and largest part of the story. As in Caravaggio's composition, Montaigne proceeds to focus closely on a central core of meaning: the protagonist about to experience revelation. In this sense, he too is situated "at the very hub of all the turmoil." In order to "spy closely on himself" ("s'espier de pres"), Montaigne must become an outsider to himself. On the other hand, if he is to describe pyschologically and physically what it feels like to die, he must remain conscious of the whole array of subjective reactions and thoughts that justify telling the tale. In fact, his "out-of-body experience" is what sets this event apart from an ordinary forensic case, and is what must subsequently be interpreted as a kind of religious experience in order to merit publication. Accordingly, the entire central core of this episode is expanded out of proportion to any natural temporal reality, as the narrator swoops in and out of the imaginary picture frame, supplying all manner of details about his own physical appearance and feeling, right down to a progress report on his internal injuries, even his thoughts while unconscious and those of others. This is an impossible proposition for any mortal, of course, and especially under the guise of an objective report. We have to keep in mind that this is neither fiction nor poetry. What began as a transcendance of mind over matter, as Montaigne paints the scene for the spectator, has become a virtuoso performance of multiple perspectives, with the author everywhere at once, exploring every conceivable angle.

The commentary is further complicated by a lack of linear progression. As a literary simulation of the state of semi-consciousness it de-

[5] *Acts* 9:7: "And the men which journeyed with him stood speechless, hearing a voice, but seeing no man."

scribes, the text mirrors its own subject, drifting back and forth between philosophical reflection (theory), description of actual events (practice), and their simultaneous interpretation (synthesis).[6] When the story line is picked up after an interruption, it often doubles back to restate what has been told otherwise, or to reflect on another aspect of it before continuing. In essence, Montaigne appears to replicate, consciously or not, Luke's own literary technique of supplying different but complementary details in each of three accounts of the same conversion. Through a cumulative fusion of the three versions, Luke transforms what he introduced as a traditional healing narrative into a commissioning narrative, supplying bit by bit the information needed to understand the purpose of Paul's violent encounter.[7] The three days during which Paul remained "blind" in a house in Damascus are usually interpreted as a spiritual apprenticeship, a time during which the catechumen purified himself in preparation for the sacrament of communion. In this in-between state, Paul was assumed to be receiving spiritual nourishment, and so accepted neither food nor drink. Erasmus, whose *Paraphrases on Acts* Montaigne most likely knew from an early age (cf. Trinquet), inserts the following interpretation into his summary of *Acts* 9:

> Saul, recovering himself, arose: the first step to virtue is to stand erect. Behold, again, a second miracle—though his eyes were open, he saw nothing! His companions therefore led him by the hand into the city of Damascus. He was not at once admitted to the gift of the Holy Spirit, in order to offer a prescriptive example to coming generations: the laying on of hands should not be administered to just anyone immediately, but catechumens should first be tested and prepared by fasting and prayer. Therefore, just as the apostles had remained in Jerusalem for ten days awaiting the Holy Spirit, so Saul remained in Damascus for three days. He saw nothing with the eyes of the body, but the eyes of his mind were meanwhile enlightened. He ate nothing, but his soul in the meantime was fattened on heavenly doctrine. (Erasmus 64)

[6] L. Marin has compared the elliptical nature of the language and the narrative structure itself to a "syncope" (black-out), and we might add, by analogy to the presumed Biblical prototype, an eclipse, a blind-spot or dark-spot.

[7] Hamm (66-67) develops the aspect of gradual unfolding as characteristic of Luke's design.

By the time Paul regains his sight and strength, he is prepared to receive the Holy Spirit, a kind of second sight, and begin his mandate of witnessing to others. In one variant, however, Paul experiences a second Christophany before he is confirmed in his mission.

Montaigne's tale at first seems to be winding up in similar fashion. He is carried home in the arms of his farmhands (we note that the laying on of hands is a classical motif) and offered remedies (of which he took none), but it is clear that his spirit has not yet reintegrated his body: "I was not there at all," states the continuously-expanding metatext, "These were idle thoughts, in the clouds, set in motion by the sensations of the eyes and ears; they did not come from within me. I did not know, for all that, where I was coming from or where I was going,..." He alludes to the weakness of his understanding of death. Gradually, however, he comes to prefer the "infinite sweetness" of the "other world," effectively renouncing earthly ties in his acceptance of death. It is at this point that the journey is complete, and he begins to revive:

> When I came back to life and regained my powers, ...I felt so bad two or three nights after that I thought I was going to die all over again,... and I still feel the effect of the shock of that collision.

At the end of the experience, then, and the end of its narration, the author will once again turn back to relive in another form the violent event that began his travel story. In true narcissistic fashion, the text doubles back on itself, closing the loop and beginning where it started, thematically and structurally, but with a difference. Thus "converted," (we should recall here that, etymologically, conversion means turning with or toward something) the same story moves up a notch, hermeneutically speaking, just as the spiral columns of Bernini's *baldachino* in St. Peter's wind their way around and up toward heaven in a never-ending motion. And, perhaps through having lived it and studied it and even savored the passage, the narrator/traveller will now truly emerge from the darkness of ignorance and "see the light":

> ...the last thing I was able to recover was the memory of this accident; I had people repeat to me several times where I was going, where I was coming from,...As for the manner of my fall, they

> concealed it from me and made up other versions for the sake of the man who had been the cause of it. But a long time after, and the next day, when my memory came to open up and picture to me the state I had been in at the instant I had perceived that horse bearing down on me (for I had seen him at my heels and thought I was a dead man,...) it seemed to me that a flash of lightning was striking my soul with a violent shock, and that I was coming back from the other world.

By the time we hear this last phrase, so imperceptibly has the text been slipping in and out of focus, and so artful have been the transitions between objective and subjective accounts, between theory and practice, that we are no longer capable of determining exactly where or what that "other world" is. Taken literally, this sentence means that the collision, which transposed him from a state of consciousness of material reality into a state of oblivion of that reality, was an illumination in which the normal values we attach to "this world" and "the other world" have been reversed. Is this another instance of baroque "short-circuiting" (logical *lapsus*)? Has the author forgotten that the shock sent him into the other world in the first instance, that this is an altered replica of the first account, or has he himself succumbed to the illusion of the two-sided mirror? It appears to be merely an "oversight," but the revealing phrase speaks eloquently of a state of mind which includes all of the above options and more. Montaigne thinks first in images, as most poetic temperaments do, and the expression his thoughts take are rarely contrived but rather naturally concrete, often physical and visual, palpable at their best. Here we are provided with an example of what the earlier critics of the baroque described as "incarnation," that is to say, the metaphorical transformation of abstract realities into tactile form.[8] Clearly he has experienced a life-altering event, and judging from the faithfulness with which his story parallels the Lucan model in *Acts*, it does seem that some sort of identification is being attempted. When Montaigne refers to St. Paul explicitly, or merely quotes him (never acknowledged), it is almost invariably in connection with the curse of man's vanity. What does not benefit the salvation of mankind but only that of an individual is

---

[8] Among others, Buffum: the "tendency to express intangible ideas in concrete form,"... "imagery, which though expressing abstract ideas retains its full physical effect;" ... "multiple-sense imagery" (27).

considered vain. Is it any surprise then, if Montaigne concludes the story of his fall with these reflections?

> This account of so trivial an event would be rather pointless, were it not for the instruction that I have derived from it myself; ... And yet,... What is useful to me may also by accident be useful to another.

If we now look at Caravaggio's Paul, we cannot help but notice the intensity of interiorized experience which has been expressed through close examination of physical detail. In particular, Paul's tensed fingers have all the appearance of divining rods and his open, outstretched arms are almost visibly pulsating as the electric shock of God's presence courses through his veins. And yet, his face is serene, betraying no emotion, and the stillness contrasts this description of the scene with all previous ones. More importantly, the absence of passion gives the impression that what we see is the objective description of an event. As with Montaigne, who likewise focused closely on his body, his sword and belt, his blood-stained doublet, his fingernails, his outstretched arms, all the action is taking place under the surface; invisible reality made physical. It has often been remarked about this painting that the sharp close-up on the central core of figures, reduced to a bare minimum, not to mention the theatrical and surprising foreshortening of the protagonist, has the effect of intensifying the drama of the scene, which is here almost clinical in its precision (e.g. *Regards sur la peinture* 18). But it is also true that the narrator has made this choice for us by not allowing any extraneous details to distract from these figures. Our reading is in this first instance controlled and determined by the narrator's perspective. If we compare this to two earlier versions of the *Conversion*, it is clear that the spectator previously enjoyed the freedom of reading the scene almost synchronically [Figs. 2 and 3]. In addition to the figuration of Paul's companions, their horses and even the source of the blinding light (God), we are shown the whole scene instead of an enlarged fragment—as is the case in Caravaggio's *Conversion*. And while it is never possible to take in an image all at once, Renaissance artists before Caravaggio had always attempted to render a literal account of the Scriptures. I see an analogous treatment to Caravaggio's in Montaigne's greatly-magnified central description of his in-between state, and in the unnatural angles of vision we (and he) must imagine to follow the description of the event. The mental gymnastics required to visualize the collision alone, as he simultaneously perceives the horse bearing down on him and at his heels—while the reader/spectator must first see him from behind—almost defy imagination.

There are a great many other similarities between their rhetorical techniques, not the least of which is the process of dialectical opposition—clearly a characteristic of the baroque mentality. In Caravaggio, this results in strong contrasts, be it dark and light or dividing the canvas into antithetical, reflecting but different halves. In this painting, both Paul and the horse absorb and refract the supernatural light, one onto another. Some consider that the horse represents terrestial qualities and Paul the celestial, and so forth (*ibid.*). Structurally, each completes the arc described by the silhouette of the other (Bonsanti 44). If this is not totally clear, Caravaggio's *Narcissus* (Fig. 4) should be proof-positive of the baroque obsession with cissiparity. In Montaigne, dialectical opposition results in a groping, halting progression, apparent on every textual level. It also means, in the essay in question, that the account must be continually broken down into opposing considerations in order to grasp all aspects of the truth and arrive at a synthesis. The narrative—necessarily linear—more properly resembles a zigzag, or spiral, than a straight line. Thus, the story of Montaigne's fall consists of three parts: a statement, a contrary proposition or description, and the modified re-statement. In terms of content, these three divisions are: the uninformed description of the accident (first death), the intermediary state (study and preparation), and the enlightened re-statement (second death and simultaneous rebirth). Significantly, it is only after observing "death" first hand that the narrator is able to die a second time, seeing the light, and be reborn.

In both writer and painter, the isolation and dilation of the very instant of transitional passage serves to pluck its subject out of the temporal flow of humanity. Cast in this new light, these subjects become exemplary, immortal.[9] Both Caravaggio and Montaigne have orchestrated these effects consciously. Just what they inherited from Luke's

[9] G. Kennedy identifies a distinctive rhetoric of religion based on authoritative proclamation, not rational persuasion. The phenomenon known as "sacred language" counts among its distinguishing characteristics statements which are "imagistic and metaphorical, lending the reality of sensory appearances a new meaning," but its pronouncements are also "outside of time." (6).

interpretation of the conversion/call in the *Acts* is open to discussion, but what they both share with the evangelist is a manner, typically baroque in my opinion, of imposing a specific path of reading. The appropriation and management of interpretive choices is a moral criterion of composition, and amounts to another form of didacticism. By fragmenting and carefully arranging access to information, both narrators control the progressive birth of meaning, and the reader, in order to grasp the message, must assimilate all the pieces that make it up, in the right order (Bonsanti 32-33). This does not mean that there is only one correct reading, or one narrative path that yields meaning; further, it does seem true that cultural artifacts from periods of transition have a special power to generate multiple interpretations. Rather, it is important to decipher which path the author felt was exemplary. For this reason, caution should be exercised when drawing conclusions about the meaning of such diverse representations of the conversion as we have seen in Montaigne and Caravaggio. But the techniques of composition among the different arts, the paths of signifying that might distinguish baroque from other mentalities, still remain wide open for study.

WORKS CITED

Bonsanti, Giorgio. *Le Caravage*. Firenze: Scala, 1984.
Buffum, Imbrie. *Studies in the Baroque from Montaigne to Rotrou*. New Haven: Yale UP, 1957.
Erasmus, Desiderius. *Paraphrase on the Acts of the Apostles*. Ed. J. Bateman. Trans. Robert D. Sider. Toronto: U of Toronto P, 1995.
Frame, Donald (trans.). *The Complete Essays of Montaigne*. 3 vols. Garden City NY: Doubleday, 1960.
Friedlaender, Walter. *Caravaggio Studies*. Princeton: Princeton UP, 1955.
Hamm, Dennis. "Paul's Blindness and Its Healing: Clues to Symbolic Intent" *Biblica* 71/1 (1990): 63-72.
Hedrick, Charles W. "Paul's Conversion/Call: A Comparative Analysis of the Three Reports in Acts." *Journal of Biblical Literature* 100/3 (1981): 415-32.
Kennedy, George. *New Testament Interpretation through Rhetorical Criticism*. Chapel Hill: The University of North Carolina Press, 1984.

Marin, Louis. "Montaigne's Tomb, or Autobiographical Discourse," *Oxford Literary Review* 3 (1981): 43-58.
Meyer, Marvin W. "The Light and Voice on the Damascus Road" *Forum* 2 (1986): 27-35.
Montaigne, Michel de. *Essais*. Ed. P. Villey et V. L. Saulnier. Paris: Presses Universitaires de France, 1965.
Regards sur la peinture, 13 (*Le Caravage*), Paris: Editions Fabbri, 1988.
Stanley, David. M. "Paul's Conversion in Acts: Why the Three Accounts?" *Catholic Biblical Quarterly* 15 (1953): 315-38.
Trinquet, Roger. "Les deux sources de la morale et de la religion chez Montaigne," *Bulletin de la Société des Amis de Montaigne* 13 (1968): 24-33.

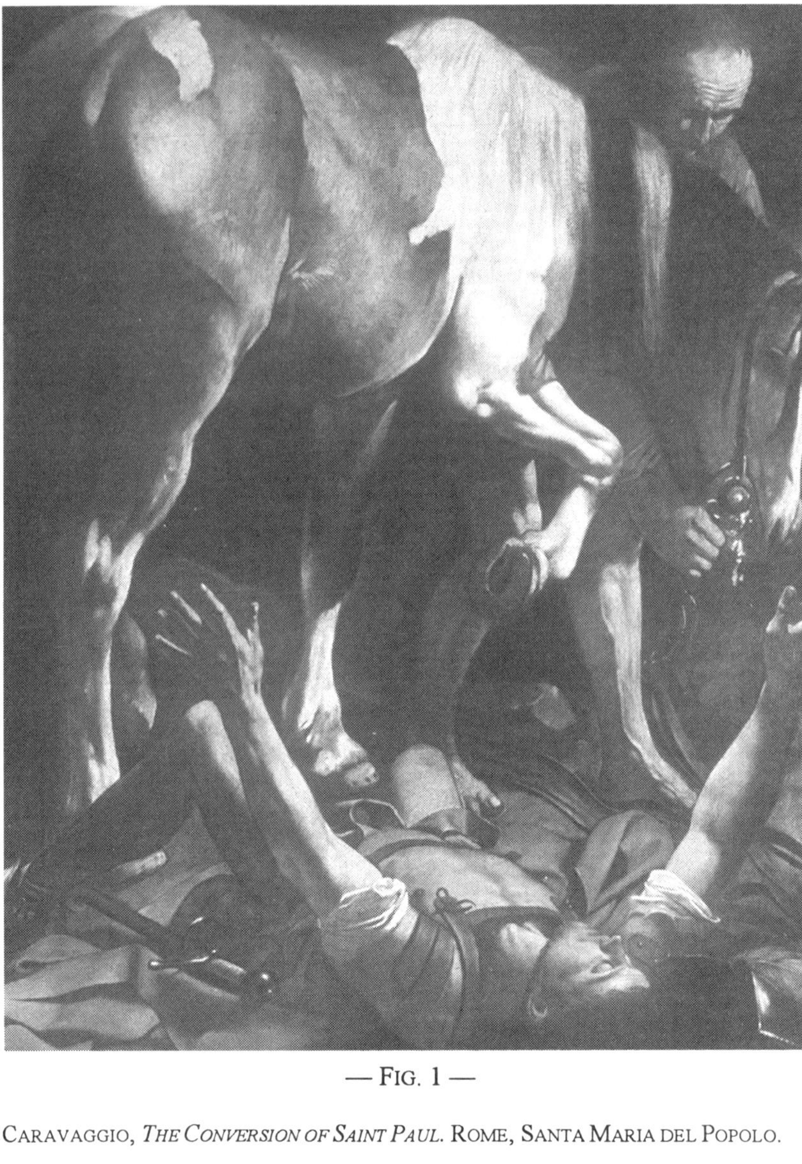

— FIG. 1 —

CARAVAGGIO, *THE CONVERSION OF SAINT PAUL*. ROME, SANTA MARIA DEL POPOLO.

— FIG. 2 —

RAPHAEL, *THE CONVERSION OF SAINT PAUL* (TAPESTRY). ROME, VATICAN.

— FIG. 3 —

MICHELANGELO, *THE CONVERSION OF SAINT PAUL*. ROME, PAULINE CHAPEL.

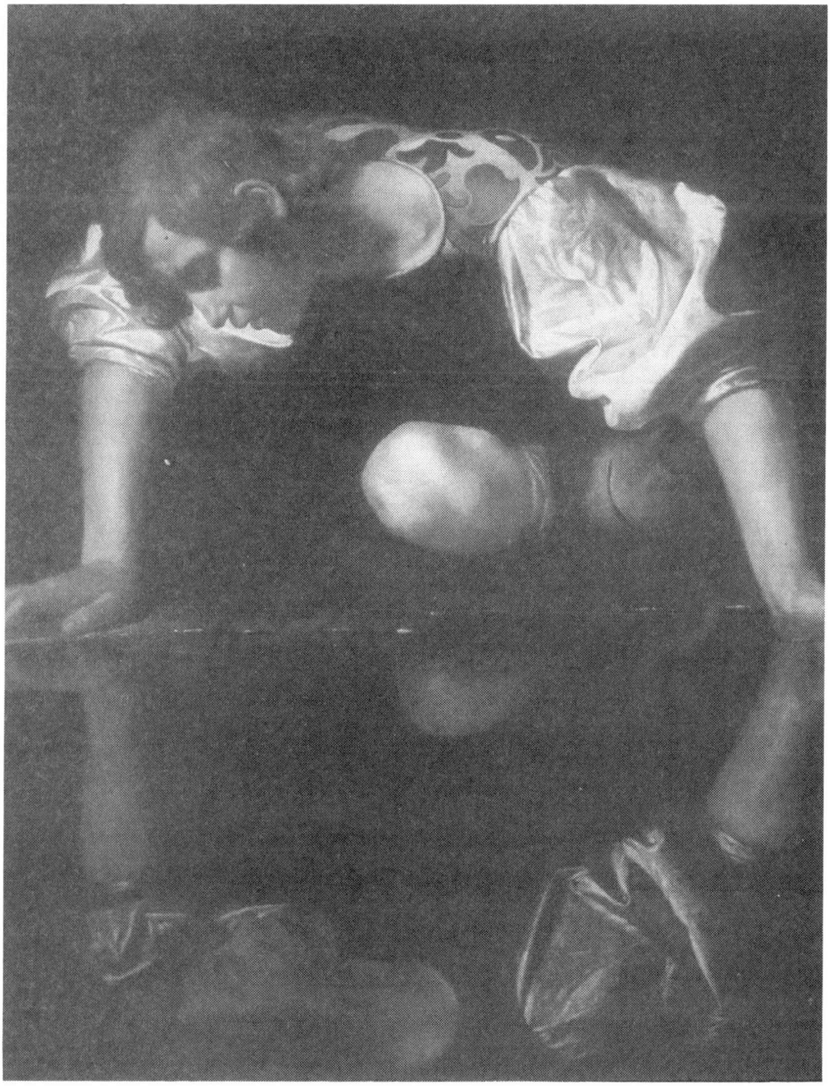

— FIG. 4 —

CARAVAGGIO (ATTR.), *NARCISSUS*. ROME, GALLERIA NAZIONALE.

Ann Dooley

More Broke than Baroque: The Irish Perspective

ABSTRACT. This paper will explore some of the key terms, Renaissance, post-Renaissance, Reformation, Counter-Reformation, Baroque, Colonialist... by which we define the early modern period culturally in so far as these terms have their own particular Irish resonance. Neither the terms themselves nor the cultural products of the period that they aim to describe can be divorced from the political disasters that overwhelm and subsume all other realities in early modern Ireland. This paper will review the current cultural debate on the Irish seventeenth century and examine two literary figures writing in Irish, one from the beginning and one from the end of the period.

It would have been tempting indeed, as my friend and colleague David Wilson reminds me, to write the story of the Irish Baroque in musical terms, to present the extraordinary transformations effected in Irish musical history by the great figure of Carolan the harper. This is a reflection of the way in which European Baroque sensibility can, in Francesco Guardiani's terms function as cultural interface, linking the traditional and the new, and yielding as hybrid forms, the Gaelic-ornamented jigs and reels, that have since taken root as the "natural" medium of Irish and Irish-inspired music in the Old World and, most spectacularly, in the New Canadian world of east coast traditional "Celtic" music. But my métier is literature and for such as myself the term Baroque comes with a heightened degree of difficulty in its application and indeed in its very applicability. It is rather less at home for us as a critical term than it is for the art historian, the architect, or the musicologist.

As a literary term, it is also a concept that is better or more natural to think with in some European areas than others and, at first sight, the Irish setting is not promising. Indeed, the term has not hitherto

Going for Baroque: Cultural Transformations1550-1650.
A St. Michael's College Symposium. Francesco Guardiani ed. Ottawa: Legas, 1999

been used for Gaelic Ireland. Certain Baroque representational modes—one might almost say states of mind—could apply, e.g. hybridity of form, multiple effects controlled by overarching themes, a reaching for the effect of the sublime, emblematic or mythological manipulations and assemblages, and mediations of meaning that tend towards pessimism etc...A further difficulty in our use of the Baroque as a literary term is that it is not confidently fixed to any specific literary period in the British Isles. It was first suggested as a useful concept for English literary history by René Wellek, then followed up by Frank Warnke and Louis Martz. Warnke divides the period between early Baroque, which would include late sixteenth century and metaphysical poets, and High Baroque which would include figures like Crashaw and above all Marvell and Milton, and would extend into the later part of the century. Its initiation as a British art term would coincide with the art and architecture of the Guildhall and Whitehall and the English commissions of Rubens and Van Dyck. For my purposes I am going to use a kind of *translatio studii* stratagem, following the English architectural historian and conoisseur, James Lee–Milne, in assigning the years 1685-1715 to the architectural insular and to see literary Baroque reverberations in Ireland as consistent with this time–span.

But the Irish Baroque if it is to be talked about at all must struggle for some cleared ground for itself against the cultural model of the imperialism/colonialism dialectic. For the major grouping of Irish literary critics, artists, and historians, the model afforded by the Field Day Project is the critical model of choice whereby literary and historic forms of nation-making can best be understood.[1] Ideas of national identity formation from this group holds the interest of our critics and Edward Said's formulation (*Culture and Imperialism, passim*), has had enormous influence on current Irish critical writing about the conditions and predeterminations of cultural discourse in Ireland from the Tudor Period to the 20th century. If one may quote Said on the issue: "In an important sense, we are dealing with the formation of cultural identities understood not as essentialisations

[1] The dominant thinker here has been Seamus Deane and his views are succintly expressed in his *A Short History of Irish Literature*, his various editorials in *The Crane Bag*, running from 1997 to 1984, and indirectly in the new series of Field Day Monographs, 1995 to 1998.

(though this is part of their enduring appeal) but as contrapuntal ensembles, for it is the case that no identity can exist by itself and without an array of opposites, negatives, oppositions: Greeks always require barbarians...[and in this case, as Arnold pleaded, Empire needs Celts][2]...In British culture one may discover a consistency of concern that fixes socially empowered space in metropolitan England and connects it by design, motive and development to distant or peripheral worlds (Ireland, Venice, Africa, Jamaica), conceived of as desirable, but subordinate." (Said, 60-1)

The shadow of British nation-making and in particular of English self-fashioning looms large over any effort to view the Irish culture world on its own terms from the end of the sixteenth century. Greenblatt's formulation of Renaissance self-fashioning and his examination of Spenser's use of Ireland in *The Faerie Queene* shows how vital the colonised is to the coloniser, and it has become almost impossible to accord this work a reading which will avoid the issue of overt propagandist aims, even in its purest poetasting modalities (Greenblatt, 157-92). Without the presence of the supine barbarian "other" no "imperial self" and no major discursive literary mode can be constructed. One can no longer separate the undertaker who espouses the harshest of colonialist methods of dealing with the native in *A Short View of the Present State of Ireland*, and the major English Renaissance romancier of *The Faerie Queene*.

This may well be an appropriate point to consider one of the most famous—indeed infamous—Spenserian moments of presenting the Irish "Other." It may also serve to open the literary debate on the status of the Baroque as a phase of Renaissance myth-making and poetic construction. The passage is implicated in the problematics of post–Renaissance discourse about man and his world of Discoveries—here couched in Final Solutions to the native problem. At the same time it uses a discourse which might be said to mark the instability of the New Europe's ability to fashion a rhetoric, an answerable style, for the more "unspeakable" underside to the inheritors of the Age of Discoveries. Midway in the Dialogue Eudoxius raises, only to dismiss, the question of compassion and Irenius replies:

---

[2] Bracketed interjection is my own extrapolation.

> ....by this hard restraint they would quickly consume themselves, and devoure one another. The proofe wherof, I saw sufficiently exampled in these late warres of Mounster, for notwithstanding that the same was a most rich and plentifull countrey, full of corne and cattle, that you would have thought they shouldhave been able to stand long, yet ere one yeare and a halfe they were brought to such wretchednesse, as that any stony heart would have rued the same. Out of every corner of the woods and glynnes they came creeping forth upon their hands, for their legges would not beare them; they looked like anatomies of death, they spake like ghosts crying out of their graves; they did eate the dead carrions, happy where they could finde them, yea, and one another soone after, insomuch as the very carcasses they spared not to scrape out of their graves; and, if they found a plot of water-cresses or shamrocks, there they flocked as to a feast for the time, yet not able long to continue therewithall; that in short space there were none almost left, and a most populous and plentifull countrey suddainely left voide of man and beast; yet sure in all that warre, there perished not many by the sword, but all by the extremitie of famine, which they themselves had wrought.
>
> Eudoxius: It is a wonder that you tell, and more to bee wondred how it should so shortly come to passe (Hadfield and Maley, 101-2).

The passage well exemplifies the difficulty which a figure such as Spenser, at once litterateur and politic man, has in applying a colour of rhetoric, a literary gloss, to some of the more unsavoury aspects of the Baroque imperializing enterprize. The value of the Spenser /Irenius contribution is that he is a historical witness to the events that he describes, thus the scoping of this traumatic passage implicates Spenser himself as the authoratitive point-of-view; indeed, after this passage Irenius as much as admits that the English military scorched-earth policy of Lord Grey is as much implicated as Irish rebellion in the devastation of Munster.[3] Spenser's rhetoric struggles mightily for control of the agenda by using fairly typical seventeenth-century terms that emphasise the attempt to remove the rawness of the scene

[3] Hadfield and Maley's edition discusses the latest controversies on Spenser and Ireland with ample bibliographical detail. For further recent excellent dicussions on Spenserian poetics, politics and Ireland, see Baker, Highley, King and Wood, *passim*.

by rendering it emblematic... "exampled," "anatomies," "a wonder..." The green world of Munster is viewed as a natural world gone hideously wrong. In the agenda of conquest and colonization the aboriginals trapped in nature outside the safe zone of the imperial garrison become subsumed into nature and become unnatural; they eat grass and devour each other; they importune the viewer for mercy with gesture and voice but they are not heard. Spenser, the imperial administrator and new Renaissance élite man retreats into the defensive thickets of overarching policy–speak and literary renderings of strange effects; he hopes they will compose themselves quietly into the quiescent forms of a neat woodcut illustration as "anatomies of death;" they are at best, as one commentator calls them, "self-consuming artifacts," at their least meaningful, a sanitary problem for the conquistador surveyer as he assumes control of the landscape. It is this discursive tension between the "discource of wonder," the unmediated reportage of the discoverer in the land of the barbarian and the forcefulling controlling and shaping eye of the Renaissance civilizer that constitutes the interest of the scene. It is a powerfully two-faced passage that serves its own emblematic function for us as representing the position of Ireland in the drama of unfolding seventeenth–century accounts of the nature of the body politic and of civility.

To begin with Spencer like this is to signal the kinds of challenge there is in providing a literary "other" against which the dominant modes of native Irish literary figuration can be assessed. The great figures from English literature, Spencer, Shakespeare, Marvell and Milton all address the Irish question in one way or another and how they treat the matter of Ireland is intimately bound up with the developing concept of Britain and of the United Kingdom as inclusive terms of nationhood.

I have already said that the main value of siting the Baroque in a mixed literary/political context is that it is the only way in which Irish literary history can be written. To use Baroque in this way has the virtue of convenience and the term can then describe a period of enormous transitional significance for Irish history and literature. It is this period that sees the creation of the Jacobite cause in European culture and marks the second phase of Irish historical re–insertion into the affairs of Europe in that long and disastrous Irish seventeenth century. Indeed, we might go farther: it is the bold contention of Breandán O Buachalla's recent magisterial study of the Gaelic poets of the period that it is Jacobitism that created the Irish nation as we know it today: that the cultural forms of Gaelic Jacobitism are the only possible conduits of a form of otherness, of resistance to the Imperial British design in Ireland; that they are the only form that was capable of transcending all class distinctions and interests, that with Jacobitism critical hegemonic mass—to use Gramscian terms—was achieved.[4] Through this critical massing achieved by Jacobitism it was virtually dictated that Irish national expressiion would realise its highest valency through Gaelic and counter–Reformation modes. Through the forms of Jacobitism, a separate and irreconcilable Irishness could flow on into the Messianic modes of the later eighteenth and early nineteenth century. Furthermore, Jacobitism, our Baroque, assumed a purely discursive form in Ireland with no culture of the decorative artifacts of Jacobitism such as obtained in England and Scotland. This in itself has had a profound influence on how we understand and mediate cultural meaning to this day in Ireland. The Yeatsian formula "Words alone are certain good" is then a particularly Irish slant on culture, and expresses the essence of the Jacobite inheritance.[5]

It would seem appropriate then that we try to understand how the historical conditions that produced the Gaelic literature of the period, the patrons and audience for whom it was written, the poets themselves, and finally those characteristics of the poetic corpus, can fruitfully answer to the term Baroque as I have historicised or, indeed, politicised it.

First, the European dimension: The reign of James II, 1695-89, was for Ireland a time of immense hope, a time when it was possible to dream again of a more total restoration of the old land ownership that obtained before the terrible wars of the hundred years before had destroyed the Gaelic and Old English hegemony, a time to reap the harvest of the strenuous counter–Reformation efforts which had kept the old faith alive. It is in this milieu in 1685 that the first distinct literary history of Ireland, *Ogygia*, is published in London by Roderick

[4] For the deployment of a Gramscian analysis in reading Irish literature see Cairns and Richards *passim*.

[5] Ó Buachalla does not attempt to discuss Irish Jacobite poetry in the more specifcally literary terms of which I offer a brief sampling in this paper

O'Flaherty and dedicated to James II as Duke of York.[6] The preface is passionate in its protestation of loyalty to the Stuart line but it is primarily offered to the Catholic Stuart prince in the hopes that he will restore the lost landed estates of his family.

Our interest in its literary Baroqueness resides in the construct of the Preface. There was no frontispiece to the volume, the normal locus of figurations of the personified and allegorized state; instead O'Flaherty brings forward the dominant figure of seventeenth-century Irish political rhetoric, the figure of Ireland as a national feminine symbol. But here she is hybrid in ways she would not have been before: she is both Renaissance–Sybilline and biblical, yet she also belongs to one of the oldest nativist models for representing the land of Ireland.

> Ireland, the most ancient cradle of your forefathers, O most victorious duke, in the publication of her Antiquities implores most humbly your Grace's patronage.....with ashes strewn on her head, her loins girded with a hair–shirt, her loosened hair hanging down her face, and with tears in her eyes; and in her outstretched hands she proffers a book in which are written, *Lamentations, mourning and woe* (Ezek. 2: 10). (Quoted in Leersen, 280, his translation)

In a century which has seen the birth of the great print projects of nationalist histories in Europe, projects conceived equally for Ireland by her scattered élite, but which never saw the light of print, this volume did make it to the centre, to London. It releases itself into the mainstream of the Three Kingdom's mythmaking in print at the same time as it co–opts and recuperates the Stuart myth of Irish origins on behalf of the Gaelic need to be heard. Literary projects then are more nakedly politically needy and exigent in Ireland than they need to be elsewhere in greater Europe.

Ireland's hope in the Stuarts should have been crushed by the historical outcome of the "War of the Foreign Kings," 1689-94, but instead the Jacobite cause metamorphosed into a ceaseless expectation of reversal, a psychosis of endlessly deferred political desire. Between 1691-1745 it is estimated that 450,000 Irish left the country and went

[6] Leersen's discussion of the Irish literary politics of the seventeenth century provides the best account to date of *Ogygia* and its context; see especially 254-93.

into exile on the Continent. Ó Buachalla gives the figure (213), but it appears excessively high. The Irish constituted the most loyal core of James II's court at St. Germain, and their regiments formed the hard core of the military professional armies of both Louis XIV and later Marie Therese of Austria. One such distinguished military exile was Justin MacCarthy, brother of the head of the clan MacCarthy and descendant of the ancient kings of Munster who had reigned by the calculation of medieval Irish genealogists for some thousand years before the birth of Christ. His family constituted one of the strongest focusses of patronly expectations for the poets of the period so it is of some interest to us to see something of the character of such an Irishman at the very point when his landed interest in the country of his forefathers is at the point of extinction. This is his last will and testament:

> I, Justin MacCarthy, Lord Viscount Mountcashel, Baron of Castle Inchy and Blarney, Duke of Clancarthy, Lieutenant–General in the army of H.M. the King of France and Navarre, and Commander of the Regiments of the Irish Brigade...I desire that my body may be buried in Ireland, if it is possible for my dear and well–beloved wife, Arabella Wentworth–Strafford, to have it taken over to my family burial–ground here. I also ask her to have prayers offered for the repose of my soul. Having no longer any wealth, since my property was confiscated by the English, I can only now dispose of my name and these titles, which I hold from His Majesty King James II. Wishing to perpetuate this name and these titles, and it not being God's will to grant me any children, I give and bequeath them, for him and all his descendants, the issue of lawful marriage, to my well–beloved cousin, Florence...I counsel Florence to bear these titles with honour, and to endeavour by all means to reconquer what the English have taken from our family; and to devote himself to the service of the Stuarts and of His Majesty the King of France and Navarre, his legimate Sovereigns... (quoted in Ó Buachalla, 188, n.679)

His wife did not feel as strongly as he the burden of his heritage and so on his death in 1694 he was buried where he died in Switzerland. In Ireland, however, he was lamented in death by a number of his family poets who dipped into the ancient referential values of the keening goddesses of the land of Munster set here in symbolic formation on the borders of the territory:

In the distance is heard the keening of women-
how bitter it is to hear the cries-
keening MacCarthy of the sword,
four keens all blending together.

The cry of a woman from Cork of the harbors,
a cry from Fermoy in the North,
a cry from Ballinahinch of the ships,
and a weeping woman from Kinsale.

The cause of their grief-alas, the pity of it-
that the heroic lord of mighty Cashel,
the battle–hound of the land of Ireland
has fallen in the service of great Louis.

The pearl of Ireland, the bridegroom of Munster,
the lovely phoenix of Eibhir most renowned,
now alone in the barracks of his tomb,
the hero Justin, son of Donncha of Coole.
(Quoted in Ó Buachalla, 188-9)[7]

As with most of the great Irish landowners, loyalty to king and religion for this family resulted in dispossession and exile. It led among the poets to a profound sense of absence at the heart of their own discourse, an absence that transformed itself into the messianic and visionary strain of the longing for the deliverer, be he exiled Irish lord or Stuart king. Though it must be said that the poets of South Munster—and this despite their constant complaints of rejection and poverty—did not seem to lack for lesser landowner patrons is clear from the careers of most of them. The poet Aogán O Rathaille, who will be our focus presently and whose career spans the Baroque period exactly, has an output divided evenly between a poetry of local engagement and a poetry of general Jacobite articulation.

It is impossible to convey much about the work of Ó Rathaille in the scope of this paper. I think it best to concentrate on what I would consider makes him a Baroque cousin "by the link" so to speak. His material is almost entirely traditionally based; Ireland is the desolate woman, the forsaken bride who longs for the return of the old landowners and by extension the Stuarts who represent the only right or-

[7] The poem occurs in MS RIA 23 G 9, 3.327. The translation is my own.

der in their universe. This mythos of the *hieros gamos* is as old as the first written literature in Ireland in the seventh century. What makes Ó Rathaille's expression of it Baroque is not just the obvious decor, the reliance on Sybilline figures, the staged arrangment of divine panoramas, the introduction of calssical divinities; it resides rather in the extent of his commitment to the allegorical process, the language of visionary rapture, the barely repressed hysteria attendant on its messianic strain, and, more fundamentally still, the manner in which the basic mythos is undercut by anxieties about the validity of the allegorical process itself. Here he joins, I think a Reformation / counter-Reformation debate tradition on the ethics of the imagination as registered in metaphor and allegory. Most acutely perhaps in Spenser, the Protestant debate on images places the poet in the difficult position of steering a path between the validity of dealing in true images and the seduction and danger of their demonic falsifications. The trouble for Ó Rathaille is that the old serpent of deceit may lie at the very heart of the only imagistic model accessible to him, that of the *hieros gamos*. To put it in a Reformation way, the woman clothed with the sun must stand very close to the whore of Babylon on her multi–progenied and mouthed Blatant Beast.

Bearing this anxiety of the Baroque image in mind it may be of interest to look briefly at Ó Rathaille's most famous visionary poem, *Gile na Gile* ("Brightness of Brightness"), from the crucial Jacobite year of 1715, to get a sense of the particular problematics of the Baroque mode in Gaelic poetry:

> Brightness of brightness I beheld on the desolate way,
> crystal of crystal her blue eye rimmed in green,
> sweetness of sweetness her voice undimmed by age,
> the red and the white succeeding in her hectic cheeks.
>
> Twisting of twistings in every strand of her yellow curls
> sweeping the dew from the grass with surging movement,
> a jewel more glittering than glasssss on her high breasts,
> created at her creation in the world beyond.
>
> True tidings she brought me, she the loneliest one,
> tidings of him returning to claim his royal place,
> tidings of the crew's destruction that exiled him,
> and other truths that for sheer awe I dare not sing of.
>
> Folly of follies I came close to her,

captivated by a captive, I found myself bound fast,
I called Mary's son for help and she recoiled from me,
and vanished like a will-o-the-wisp into the fairy fort of Luachair.

I run-a crazy rout-rushing with pounding heart,
through marshes, through swamps, through barren moorland,
I reach the strong palace- I know not how ,
to that place of places created by druid magic.

Mocking they mocked me, that gang of goblins
and the band of fine wavy-tressed damzels,
In fetters they forced me with no trace of pity,
and a hidous ogre fondled my lady before me.

I told her then in plain truthful measure,
how ill it became her to mate with a salacious slob,
when the fairest man of Scotia, the three-crowned,
was waiting to wed her as his beloved bride.

At the sound of my voice she wept desolately,
the tears streamed down her hectic cheeks;
she gave me a guide to help escape the mansion,
that brightness of brightness I saw on my lonely way

Envoie

My pain, my calamity, my rack, my sorrow, my ruin!
that shining, lively, courtly, dewy-lipped lady
with one of that horned, black , evil, yellow-pated brood
and no hope of redress till the lion-heroes return over the sea.[8]

The sovereignty goddess who is Ireland herself is easily discerned here as is the underlying sexual configuration of the Jacobite political position of invocation of Stuart king and dispossessed and exiled Irish nobility. The Renaissance device of the blazon is formally deployed in quatrains 1 and 2; the woman's beauty is both natural and artificially conceptualized. She carries on her breast the great jewel which may represent the sovereignty of Ireland in another key, the great emerald whih Henry II left in Ireland in 1172 as the basis of the Irish crown jewels. The discourse of the maiden (quatrain 3) is both political news and communication of royal prophecy. In Irish tradition the

[8] Translation is my own, the text is from Ó Tuama and Kinsella, 151-2.

sign of the rightful ruler is the discernment of truth, hence the term *fios fiosach*, literally "knowledgable knowledge;" but the traditional term for truth, *fior*, is relegated here to a subsidiary role in the quatrain, serving merely as a qualifier to psychological states, "truly lonely," "true fear." Ó Rathaille's jolt to the traditional poetic system is delivered in quatrains 4-6; through the diabolic reversal and devil–testing (4), the otherworld dwelling in the liminal place and the scene of Pandemonium in quatrains 5 and 6. The poet himself then speaks in quatrain 7 and the role of truth–teller is reversed; truth–telling is now *his* business *friotal dob fhíor uaimse* ("poetry most true from me"). The poet emerges as the preacher of Jacobite political correctedness and the effect of his rhetoric is immediate; she weeps and sends him a guide to take him safely out of his state of enchantment.

Perhaps it is not too much to say that in the figure of the guide of the final quatrain can be seen the much diminished supplement of a nativist poetics; mediation between transcendent divine powers of the goddess and the human spokesperson of the gods, the poet, is reduced to a mere cipher a figure who enables the poet to return from the otherworld but who is no aid to voice, to the old nativist ability to offer at the *hieros gamos* a rich cup of truth–telling. But beyond the political problems of native Gaelic discourse there is also the difficulties of the poet and his poetics. The dilemna confronting Ó Rathaille is the same as that confronting Spenser one hundred years earlier but the fact that Ó Rathaille is writing at the end of the century causes it to be posed in even more acute terms. The Bower of Bliss, the imagining of feminized poetic transcendence, even if it represents the finest work of the sensuous imagination of the poet, must in the end be torn down.

Ó Rathaille, here and elsewhere follows his goddess to the end only to realise that that end is the irretrievable loss of the benign conditions that once favoured bright imaginings. The patrons are gone, the groves and banqueting halls deserted and the result is that, at the moment of poetic climax, the irruption of the poetic auctorial voice of moral or political correction, that attempts to assert control over the discource, merely succeeds in drawing attention to the realization that the authority of that voice may already be voided. That loss may be even more painful for Ó Rathaille than it was for Spenser; for to break or to disable the poetic mythos is to carry a grave burden. It is not just as with Spenser, the effort of forging from a single individual's own strenuous self–fashioning an effective and significant poetic voice that strives to be heard in the victorious master discourse of Britain but, in the Irish poet's case, individual voice had never before forced a break in the collective traditional utterance of a whole nation. For better or worse, however, Ó Rathaille's pessimism remained a unique experiment in the co–option of traditional Gaelic forms to the needs of individual expressiveness. Such interrogations of the communal *mythos* leading on to experiments on the level of personal heartbreak such as Ó Rathaille produced were not to be repeated again on a level of great or significant Gaelic poetry. The mould of the Gaelic mythos of sovereignty, then, proved more durable than ever Ó Rathaille dreamed of.

WORKS CITED

Baker, David J. *Between Nations: Shakespeare, Spenser, Marvell, and the Question of Britain*. Stanford: Stanford University Press, 1997.

Cairns, David, and Richards, Shaun. *Writing Ireland: Colonialism, Nationalism and Culture*. Cultural Politics. Manchester: Manchester University Press, 1988.

Deane, Seamus. *A Short History of Irish Literature*. London: Hutchinson, 1986.

Hadfield, Andrew and Maley, Willy. *Edmund Spenser: Aview of the State of Ireland.* Oxford: Blackwell, 1997.

Highley, Christopher *Shakespeare, Spenser, and the Crisis in Ireland.* Cambridge Studies in Renaissance Literature and Culture, Cambridge: Cambridge University Press, 1997.

King, John N. *Spenser's Poetry and the Reformation Tradition*. Princeton: Princeton University Press, 1990.

Leerssen, Joep. *Mere Irish and Fíor–Ghael: Studies in the Idea of Irish Nationality, its Development and Literary Expression prior to the Nineteenth Century*. Critical Conditions: Field Day Monographs. Cork: Cork University Press, 1996.

Martz, Louis, *From Renaissssance to Baroque: Essays on Literature and Art*. Columbia: University of Missouri Press, 1991.

Ó Buachalla, Breandán. *Aisling Ghéar: Na Stiobhardaigh agus an tAos Léinn, 1603-1788*. Baile Átha Cliath: An Clóchomhar Tta, 1996.

Ó Tuama, Seán, and Kinsella, Thomas. *An Duanaire, 1600-1900: Poems of the Dispossessed*. Dublin: The Dolmen Press, 1981.

Said, Edward. *Culture and Imperialism*. London: Chatto and Windus, 1993.

Warnke, Frank J. *Versions of Baroque: European Literature in the Seventeenth Century*. New Haven: Yale University Press, 1972.
Wood, Rufus. *Metaphor and Belief in the Faerie Queene*. Basingstoke and New York: Macmillan Press and St. Martin's Press, 1997.

Randall A. Rosenfeld

Van Eyck's *Der Fluyten Lust-hof* (1644-*ca.* 1655) and the Perception of the Baroque

ABSTRACT. Jacob van Eyck's anthology is the single largest collection of solo wind music published up to its time, and, as it is known that *Der Fluyten Lust-hof* represents a 'live' repertoire, it furnishes an excellent opportunity to explore the characteristics of a music which, originating in a specific place and performance situation, nevertheless reflects some international influence. Van Eyck's *Der Fluyten Lust-hof* is examined within the context of the visual arts and politics of the Dutch *"Gouden Eeuw"* (Golden Age), and the understanding of the sound, appearance, and symbolism of the Dutch Baroque which this examination offers has important implications for our perception of pan-European Baroque culture.

> *The noble-born gentleman Jacob van Eyck, a musician of wide renown and high regard, the supervisor of all the carillons and clock-work bells of the cathedral and city of Utrecht, died on the 26th of March, 1657.*
>
> *Van Eyck, of the good family Bax, lies here interred; as God slighted his sight he enhanced his ear, made his tongue more fluent and fingers fleet to match; van Eyck, a marvel through the ages on flute, and carillon.*[1]

I wish to thank Andrea Budgey, Joe Goering, Francesco Guardiani, Giulio Silano, and Bob Sweetman for advice and assistance with this paper, and Professor Guardiani for the invitation to take part in the conference. Any errors are happily my own.

[1] The second text translated here is from a source printed the year of van Eyck's death; texts in van Baak Griffioen, *Jacob van Eyck*, 23, 39. The principal studies on van Eyck both appeared as published theses in the last decade; van den Hul, *Klokkenkunst*, and van Baak Griffioen, *Jacob van Eyck*. The first is important for the details of his career, and the second is a thorough source study

of the tunes in *Der Fluyten lust-hof*; I am indebted to both works. All translations in this text are my own, unless otherwise noted. Abbreviations used throughout are as follows:

> *Der Fluyten Lust-hof*: Jacob van Eyck, *Der Fluyten Lust-hof, vol Psalmen, Paduanen, Allemanden, Couranten, Balletten, Airs, etc.*, printed by Paulus Matthysz. (Amsterdam, 1649-1654), facsimile edition, ed. Kees Otten (Amsterdam, 1979?);
>
> de Sany, *Carillon*: *Recueil d'hymnes et chansons arrangés par Théodore de Sany pour le carillon de Bruxelles en 1648*, ed. Jean-Pierre Felix (Bruxelles, 1990), 2 vols.;
>
> Grove's *Art*: *The Grove Dictionary of Art*, ed. Jane Shoaf Turner (London, 1996);
>
> Grove's *Music and Musicians*: *The New Grove Dictionary of Music and Musicians*, ed. Stanley Sadie (London, 1980^6);
>
> *Hoogsteder*: *The Hoogsteder Exhibition of Music and Painting in the Golden Age*, Edwin Buijsen and Louis Peter Grijp *et al.* (The Hague, 1994);
>
> Israel, *Dutch Republic*: Jonathan Israel, *The Dutch Republic: Its Rise, Greatness, and Fall 1477-1806*, Oxford History of Early Modern Europe, ed. R. J. W. Evans (Oxford, 1995);
>
> *Saenredam*: Gary Schwartz and Marten Jan Bok, *Pieter Saenredam: The Painter and His Time* (New York, 1990^2);
>
> Schama, *Riches*: Simon Schama, *The Embarrassment of Riches: an Interpretation of Dutch Culture in the Golden Age* (n., 1987);
>
> *17th Century Recorder*: *The Recorder in the 17th Century: Proceedings of the International Recorder Symposium, Utrecht 1993*, ed. David Lasocki (Utrecht, 1995);
>
> van Baak Griffioen, *Jacob van Eyck*: Ruth van Baak Griffioen, *Jacob van Eyck's 'Der Fluyten Lust-hof' (1644-c1655)*, Vereniging voor Nederlandse Muziekgeschiedenis, Muziekhistoriche monografieën 13, ed. Arend Jan Gierveld (Utrecht, 1991);
>
> van den Hul, *Klokkenkunst*: Dick van den Hul, *Klokkenkunst te Utrecht tot 1700, met bijzondere aandacht voor het aandeel hierin van Jhr. Jacob van Eyck*, Vereniging voor Nederlandse Muziekgeschiedenis, Muziekhistorische monografieën 9 (Utrecht, 1982).

So van Eyck's stone told his fame to succeeding generations. In his day it was important to 'die well,' to leave a good report of one's life at one's death, to avoid shaming one's kin and circle, and to cheat oblivion. Charles, the English martyr-king, proved a virtuoso at this 'one-off' baroque art form.[2] Van Eyck's fame was as fleet as his fingers; it had crumbled long before the disappearance of his monument in the last century (Van Baak Griffioen, *Jacob van Eyck*, 39, note 47). Luck plays a part, but fame clearly offers preferrment to those in high station, actors in high tragedy whose performances are acknowledged by heavenly portents. Van Eyck's current reputation is a result of the revival of the music of his century in ours, yet the memory inscribed on his stone excites interest: a blind musician of polite birth, famed as a performer, who successfully held an involved civic office. There are strains of the universal, as well as the singular, in this tune. The blind musician is a universal type: Francesco Landini in the fourteenth century, and Conrad Paumann in the fifteenth, and they, like van Eyck, were keyboardists who also played recorders.[3] They were also

---

[2] The literature on Charles I, and his end, is vast; see Charles Carleton, *Charles I, the Personal Monarch* (London and New York, 1995^2), especially ix, 343-354, and the classic study by C. V. Wedgwood, *The Trial of Charles I* (London, 1964). The legend of Charles existed before the publication of [John Gauden,] *Eikon basilike: The pourtraicture of His sacred Maiestie in his solitudes and sufferings* (London, 1648 = 1649 new style).

[3] On Landini, see Giovanni Gherardi da Prato, *Il Paradiso degli Alberti*, ed. A. Lanza (Rome, 1975), 164 *et seq.*, and the chapter from Filippo Villani's Chronicle, *Liber de origine civitatis florentiae et eiusdem famosis civibus* (1385-1397), excerpted in F. Alberto Gallo, *Music of the Middle Ages II*, tr. Karen Eales (Cambridge, 1985), 128-129; Kurt von Fischer, 'Landini, Francesco,' in *Grove's Music and Musicians*, vol. 10, 428-434; Michael Long, 'Francesco Landini and the Florentine Cultural Élite,' in *Early Music History: Studies in Medieval and Early Modern Music*, ed. Ian Fenlon, 3 (1983), 83-99. On Paumann, see Franz Krautwurst, 'Paumann,' in *Die Musik in Geschichte und Gegenwart...*, ed. F. Blume (Kassel, Basel, London, and New York, 1962), cols. 968-971; Christoph Wolff, 'Paumann, Conrad,' in *Grove's Music and Musicians*, vol. 14, 308-309; Keith Polk, *German Instrumental Music of the Late Middle Ages: Players, Patrons and Performance Practice*, Cambridge Musical Texts and Monographs, ed. Howard Mayer Brown, Peter Le Huray, and John Stevens (Cambridge, 1992), 14-15 *et seq.*, and the bibliography cited on 216, notes 3-5.

famed as improvisers. Rarer is the professional of gentle blood; Archangelo Corelli alone comes readily to mind.[4] Van Eyck's chosen keyboard instrument, the carillon, is the particular public instrument of the Netherlands. The only direct experience we can have of van Eyck's art, and it is a simulacrum, is through the published corpus of his music. Commonly known by the collective title of its second edition, *Der Fluyten Lust-hof*, this artefact of the Dutch 'Golden Age' is an agreeable vehicle for examining some of our perceptions of the pan-European movement we call the Baroque. That is where I will end. I begin this paper with an overview of van Eyck's life and work.

Jacob van Eyck (1589/90-1657) was born about the beginning of the final decade of the sixteenth century, when the desperate military fortunes of the protestant Dutch rebels were becoming less desperate (Jonathan Isarel, *Dutch Republic*, 241-262). His home town was probably Heusden, located in the southern Dutch province of Brabant.[5] He was one of five children. His father stemmed from a bastard branch of the van Eyck's, a family numbered among the patrician gentry, but he was as well connected, if not better, through his mother, who was of the Bax family.[6] Through them he was related to the Huygens; van Eyck's maternal grandfather was brother to Constantijn Huygens' great-grandfather.[7] We will return to Constantijn Huygens (1596-1687), for he played a part in van Eyck's life, and consequently has a place in this narrative.

We know next to nothing of the musical education, or apprenticeship, Jacob van Eyck received. Blind from birth, he was compensated, as noted, with better hearing; and he was gifted with the ability to turn an acute ear to proficient music making. The possibility exists that he

[4] On Corelli, see D. Arnold *et al.*, *The New Grove Baroque Masters: Monteverdi, Frescobaldi, Cavalli, Corelli, A. Scarlatti, Vivaldi, D. Scarlatti* (London, 1984), and the prodeedings of the *Congresso internazionale di studi corelliani*, Quaderni della Rivista italiana di musicologia I (1968)-.

[5] Van den Hul, *Klokkenkunst*, 305. The family were originally from Maaseik in Limburg.

[6] Van den Hul, *Klokkenkunst*, 305. The van Eyck arms were, apparently, tierce pale raguly sable on a field d'argent.

[7] For an annotated genealogical table showing the relationship, see van den Hul, *Klokkenkunst*, 222-223.

was largely self-taught. His abilities at melodic adaptation, elaboration, variation, and implied polyphonic imitation are of a high order, yet the limited evidence of his written-out part music shows his contrapuntal style to have been un-learned.[8] The strengths and weaknesses of his music may reflect the strengths and weaknesses of his training. It is interesting that someone of his background was permitted to, or had to work as a professional musician. Many of the sons of the Dutch urban patriciate were captains of trade, or industry, rather like their counterparts in the northern Italian cities.[9] The employment they chose was invariably honourable. Few, therefore, chose to make their income through the arts; the painter Karel van Mander (1548-1606) is one of the exceptions.[10] Very few, it would seem, chose to be musicians.

[8] *Der Fluyten Lust-hof*, I, fols. 91*v*-96*r*. They are, however, rather charming in their effect. As they are less demanding than most of the diminution settings in the book, and they contain some 'illegal' progressions, van Baak Griffioen, *Jacob van Eyck*, 371, would disallow van Eyck's authorship of them. As van Baak Griffioen elsewhere in her study points to the many printing errors throughout the collection (van Baak Griffioen, *Jacob van Eyck*, 46, 61-62), it is quite likely that the errors in the duets are due to the same cause, a faulty amanuensis, rather than to van Eyck. Thiemo Wind, 'Why the Duets from *Der Fluyten Lust-hof* are not by Jacob van Eyck,' in *The Recorder Magazine* 16, no. 2 (June 1996), 44-48, also argues against van Eyck's authorship, mainly on the basis of dissimilarity of division style. Wind makes a strong case for the publisher of *Der Fluyten Lust-hof*, Paulus Matthyszoon, as the real author of the duets, and he backs this hypothesis with a good codicological observation (48). We lack, however, a sufficient body of material by Matthysz. to allow a solid analysis of his polyphonic style for comparison with the *Fluyten Lust-hof* duets. The basic *lacuna*, however, is our lack of other part-music postiviely attributable to van Eyck. If the assurance of Matthysz.' authorship can be no better than the old Scottish judgement of 'not proven,' then it is best to conserve the duets as part of van Eyck's *corpus*.

[9] I wish to thank Professor Bob Sweetman for discussion of this point.

[10] W. Waterschoot, *Ter liefde der Const: Uit het "Schilder-Boeck" (1604) van Karel van Mander*, Nijhoffs Nederlandse Klassieken, ed. J. Buijnsters *et al.* (Leiden, 1983), 3-4; for an outline of van Mander's career, and bibliography, see E. K. J. Reznicek, 'Karel van Mander,' Grove's *Art*, vol. 20, 244-249. I have been unable to consult Hessel Miedema, *Karel van Mander (1548-1606) het bio-bibliografisch materiaal verzameld door Hessel Miedema* (Amsterdam, 1972).

Van Eyck's chief professional pre-occupations were with the practice and science of campanology, clockwork-bells and carillons. His career as a player and composer-arranger of wind-music was clearly an adjunct to this. In 1625 he became carillonneur of the Utrecht *Dom*, and in 1628 he was appointed to the obligations, rights, and pleasures of the supervisor of all the 'programmable' and keyboard bells, ecclesiastical and civic, in Utrecht (Van den Hul, *Klokkenkunst*, 145; van Baak Griffioen, *Jacob van Eyck*, 28-29). This embraced responsibility for the mechanisms in the *campanili* of at least the Buurkerk[11], Nicolaikerk , Jacobikerk[12], Geertekerk, and the civic hall, as well as the *Dom*.[13] This did not, however, mean that van Eyck was *ipso facto* carillonneur of all these institutions; the office of carillonneur was a separate appointment in each, and van Eyck held at least four of these: the *Dom* (1625), Janskerk (1632)[14], Jacobikerk (1645), and the civic hall (1645), (Van den Hul, *Klokkenkunst*, 145; van Baak Griffioen, *Jacob van Eyck*, 29; 28). In addition to selecting the repertoire for the automated clockwork-bells, and programming the mechanisims to perform that repertoire, it was probable that van Eyck performed a seasonally fluctuating *cursus* of hour long recitals at each

[11] An image form later in the century is Antoni Waterlo, *Panorama of the Buurkerk and Surroundings in Utrecht*, Amsterdam, Rijksprentenkabinet, Rijksmuseum, reproduced in Richard J. Wattenmaker *et al.*, *Opkomst en bloei van het Noordnederlandse stadsgezicht in de 17de eeuw/ The Dutch Cityscape in the 17th Century and Its Sources* (Amsterdam, Toronto, 1977), cat. no. 94. On Waterlo, see B. J. Broos, 'Waterlo, Antoni,' in Grove's *Art*, vol. 32, 907-908.

[12] An interior depiction is Pieter Jansz. Saenredam, *Choir of the St. Jacobskerk, Utrecht, from South to North*, 1642, Munich, Bayerische Staatsgemäldesammlungen (Alte Pinakothek), reproduced in *Saenredam*, fig. 177, cat. nr. 134. On Saenredam, see *Saenredam*; Walter Liedtke, 'Pieter (Jansz.) Saenredam,' Grove's *Art*, vol. 27, 507-511.

[13] The bells are just visible in Pieter Jansz. Saenredam, *The Oude Gracht with the Domtoren, Utrecht*, 1636, Utrecht, Gemeentelijke Archiefdienst, Topografische Atlas, reproduced in *Saenredam*, fig. 171, cat. nr. 115.

[14] An image of part of the interior is Pieter Jansz. Saenredam, *Nave and Choir of the St. Janskerk, Utrecht, from West to East, with a view into St. Anthony's Chapel*, Rotterdam, Museum Boymans-van Beuningen, reproduced in *Saenredam*, fig. 214, cat. nr. 138.

institution of which he was carillonneur. The core of the clockwork-bell and carillon repertoire would be the melodies of the Calvinist psalter.[15]

The only professional wind playing of van Eyck's of which we are informed is his evening out-of-doors performances in the Janskerkhof. This church garden was a public garden, a fashionable spot for well-off urban youth of both sexes. Van Eyck received a raise from the Janskerkhof authorities in 1649 for providing this service, but nearly a decade earlier his musical presence had been noted as a chief attraction of an evening in the Janskerkhof.[16] Aside from his work as a performer and clockwork-bell supervisor, van Eyck also taught the carillon, and he was employed by institutions beyond the borders of

[15] While it is not impossible that *Der Fluyten Lust-hof* is similar in its range of pieces to van Eyck's carillon repertoire, few traces of which remain (see van Baak Griffioen, *Jacob van Eyck*, 33-35), it is most unlikely that the style of his carillon settings was anything like the style of his wind settings. The earliest surviving carillon repertory, de Sany, *Carillon*, is instructive in this regard. The Calvinist hymn tunes in *Der Fluyten Lust-hof* are replaced by plainchant melodies in the de Sany book (*e.g.*, de Sany: 'Conditor alme [siderum],' I, 148, II, 2; 'Victimi [sic] pascali lauds,' I, 168, II, 10, *etc.*), but, like *Der Fluyten Lust-hof*, the de Sany collection also includes settings of secular melodies (*e.g.*, de Sany: 'Susanne ung jour,' I, 229-230, II, 41; 'Ballet du Grand Ducq,' I, 241-244, II, 47-48, *etc.*). Unlike van Eyck's wind settings, however, the de Sany carillon settings are not arranged as progressive diminutions. There are fewer broken-chord figures, less extensive quick scalar passages, and a much smaller repertoire of division figures in the de Sany settings, compared to the van Eyck. Imitation and species counterpoint, the former imperfectly possible on a solo wind instrument, the latter not at all, are, not surprisingly, features of the de Sany settings. It is further interesting to note that imitation is not a feature of the two-part settings in *Der Fluyten Lust-hof* (I, fols. 91*v*-96*r*) (though it is present in another collection in a setting which Wind believes is related to these; see 44-45 of Wind's article cited in note 10 *supra*). See notes 39, and 41 *infra*.

[16] Van Baak Griffioen, *Jacob van Eyck*, 32, 43-46. There is, unfortunately, no surviving image of this. A parallel iconography, however, is available in anon., *Comet, Flute Player, and Strolling Couple*, from Johan van Nyenborgh, *Toonneel der Ambachten: of den Winckel der Handtwercken en Konsten...* (Jacob Sipkes, Groeningen, 1659-1660), reproduced in Phillip J. Pirages *et al.*, *Phillip J. Pirages Catalogue Thirty-Nine* (1996?, McMinnville), pl. 17, no. 356.

Utrecht as what we might term a consulting engineer in the field of campanology.[17]

What were the material rewards to be expected by a blind noble musician working for the city of Utrecht? This is a difficult question to answer, for various reasons. There can't have been many like van Eyck, so there is a want of material for comparison. Up to 1628 his annual salary as carillonneur of the *Dom* was 350 *fl.*; in that year he received a raise to 500 *fl.*, and his salary waş increased by a further 100 *fl.* in 1645.[18] If one assumes he was paid only half the pre-1628 figure for each of his other carillon positions, and that the salary increase from the *Dom* in 1628 included the wages for supervising Utrecht's bells, then by 1632 van Eyck was making 675 *fl.* from these sources, and by 1645 this had increased to 1125 *fl.* This figure is conservative, and it does not include any fees for teaching separate from the wages for the supervisory or carillon posts, nor does it include any fees for consultancy paid by other institutions, occasional engagements, or income from non-musical sources.[19] If a journeyman at mid-century worked every day of the year, something which he could not, and probably would not do, he would make between 400 *fl.* and 500 *fl.* *per annum*, that is, between about 35% and 44% of the conjectural figure for van Eyck's 1645 salary.[20] During van Eyck's lifetime ordinary soldiers made a paltry 150 *fl.* *per annum*, while the captian of a merchantman could easily bring home 720 *fl.* *per annum*,

[17] Van den Hul, *Klokkenkunst*, 146-150 (teaching); van Baak Griffioen, *Jacob van Eyck*, 25-32, particularly 29-32 (engineering).

[18] Van den Hul, *Klokkenkunst*, 307-308; van Baak Griffioen, *Jacob van Eyck*, 28, note 8 (who doesn't report the 1645 increase). Isreal, *Dutch Republic*, 352, points out that the Dutch Republic experienced a general economic slump throughout the 1620s and early 1630s.

[19] For the possibility of some teaching responsibilities being included in the wage, see van den Hul, *Klokkenkunst*, 145. Income from a vicarage affiliated to the Janskerk is noted at 308.

[20] The figures in Schama, *Riches*, 167, are used as the basis for these calculations. Interestingly enough, a master carpenter in Amsterdam at the same period is recorded as making 500 *fl.* *per annum* (Schama, *Riches*, 315)., and wages in Amsterdam could exceed wages elaswhere (Israel, *Dutch Republic*, 353).

nearly five times as much as the common soldier (Israel, *Dutch Republic*, 352). By contrast, the income of rich artisans and others of the petit bougeois, Simon Schama's 'middling-sort' of people, has been estimated at between 1,500 *fl.* to 3,000 *fl. per annum* (approximately 34% to 267% more than van Eyck's conjectural 1645 salary), and this group probably included urban *predikants*, as some were making well above 1,000 *fl. per annum* in Amsterdam by 1625.[21] By even greater contrast, 'rich' household incomes were at least 10,000 *fl. per annum* (Israel, *Dutch Republic*, 635, table 35). It is quite conceiveable that van Eyck made enough to place him among the 'middling-sort' of people, yet a musician who did not have a chief position at a major court could not expect to do as well as many other professionals. Van Eyck certainly made a living wage, but it is unlikely that he did spectacularly well from his musical earnings. Difficult as it is to draw comparisons across the arts, van Eyck may have been in a financial position similar to that of the painter Pieter Jansz. Saenredam (1597-1665), a contemporary who worked for a time in Utrecht.[22]

It is only in this century that reputation and worth seem to have become inexorably pegged to net worth, or wage bracket. Our ancestors were saner.

Philips Baron van Leefdael wrote at mid-century that:

... living in the city of Utrecht, where he is engaged as organist [sic], and carillonneur, [is van Eyck,] whose name shall abide in memory everlasting; for, although he is blind, no one this century has eclipsed him on the carillon, nor on the German, or any type of flute, according

---

[21] Israel, *Dutch Republic*, 635, table 35, for household incomes, and 353 for *predikant* incomes; Schama, *Riches*, 315, for 'middling people.' The figure Schama gives for schoolmaster/*predikant* income, 200 *fl. per annum* (p. 617), which is quoted by van Baak Griffioen, *Jacob van Eyck* (p. 28, note 8), is actually the wages of a village *predikant* in 1574 (Israel, *Dutch Republic*, 353), and not the income of an urban *predikant* in 1650. It is, thus, of no value as a figure for comparison to van Eyck's income.

[22] On Saenredam's finances, see *Saenredam*, 175-179. Much more information is available on Saenredam's extra-professional sources of income than on van Eyck's, and much more is known of van Eyck's professional income than Saenredam's. Schwartz and Bok come to a more optimistic conclusion regarding levels of income over 400 *fl. per annum* than is reached here.

to the opinion of all nations, and [the judgement of] connoisseurs of music and like arts. (Text in van Baak Griffioen, *Jacob van Eyck*, 37).

Van Eyck did not want for contemporary estimation. In the poem of dedication which appears in the second edition of *Der Fluyten Lust-hof* (1646), Thomas Asselijn compares van Eyck to Orpheus (*Der Fluyten Lust-hof*, II, fol. ii *v*). Regnerus Opperveldt's poem of 1640 on the Janskerkhof, as mentioned above, singles out van Eyck's wind playing (Van Baak Griffioen, *Jacob van Eyck*, 44-45). It is van Eyck's skill as a performer, as well as the circumstances under which he worked, which excite comment. The elegies on his death say as much, and no more.[23] His compositions are not mentioned, but we should bear in mind that the craft of music was such that every performer was to some extent what we would call a composer. More surprising is the silence of these poems when it comes to van Eyck's scientific knowledge and engineering skills. An indirect reference to these is found in a letter of 1638 which René Descartes wrote to Father Marin Mersenne, to report that 'a blind man of Utrecht, highly celebrated as a musician' (*vn aueugle a Vtrecht, fort renommé pour la Musique*), had the knowlege and ability to sound each one of of the five or six partials (*sons*) of the larger of the *Domtoren* bells (*plus grosses de ces cloches*), without touching their metal, simply by intoning the particular pitch close to each great mass.[24] It is the use van Eyck made of his knowledge that is striking. He apparently determined that the partials must be as in tune as possible for a bell to sound satisfactorily, and for those partials to be in tune, the bell had to have a particular shape (Van Baak Griffioen, *Jacob van Eyck*, 31).

[23] For the texts and translations of the elegies by Lodewijk Meijer and Lambertus Sanderus, see van Baak Griffioen, *Jacob van Eyck*, 394-397.

[24] *Oeuvres de Descartes: Correspondance*, ed. Charles Adam and Paul Tannery, II (Paris, 1975^2), 329-330, *ep.* CXXXVIII, 23 août 1638. This passage occurs in the context of a continuing exchange between Descartes and Mersenne on the physical properties of echos. The instance of the blind musician form Utrecht is used by Descartes to establish his position on the propagation of sound. There remains a remote chance that the '*aueugle a Vtrecht*' is not van Eyck.

On Mersenne, see Peter Robert Dear, *Mersenne and the Learning of the Schools* (Ithaca, 1988), and *1588-1988, quatrième centenaire de la naissance de Marin Mersenne: colloque scientific international et célébration nationale* (Le Mans, 1994).

This design is said to have led to a great advance in the production of tunable bells. He frequently worked with the foremost manufacturer of bells in the Netherlands, the firm of François and Pieter Hemony. In Deventer a plaque survives, now incorporated in a recast bell, which reads: "Ps. 150: 'Praise the Lord in his sanctuaries; praise him in the firmament of his strength.' The city of Deventer had us cast in the year 1647 by Frans Hemony, on the authorization of the gentleman Jacob van Eick, and master Lugas Lennich."[25] On the other hand, as I have noted, it is to his surviving published music that van Eyck owes whatever recognition he has received in our century. What sort of work is *Der Fluyten Lust-hof*?

The building where the States General tended to meet, the Binnenhof, was originally the seat of the Counts of Holland. In the words of one recent critic: "...the rabbit warren of halls, flanking wings and outbuilding appartments that made up the Binnenhof was, like the Dutch state itself, a peculiar jumble of medieval remains, Renaissance invention and contemporary improvisation."[26] This is also an apt description of van Eyck's *Der Fluyten Lust-hof*.

Van Eyck's work saw five editions between 1644 and about 1655, all within his lifetime. No posthumous edition is known, but the discovery of other editions should not be ruled out. As a codicological artefact, *Der Fluyten Lust-hof* has one unusual point of interest, and that is its format, dubbed 'sexto-oblong' (20 cm. x 10 cm.).[27] This

[25] Text in van Baak Griffioen, *Jacob van Eyck*, 36, note 36. On the Hemony's, see Hans Klotz, 'Hemony,' in *Grove's Music and Musicians*, vol. 8, 475-476.

[26] Schama, *Riches*, 226. For a suggestive image, see anon., *The Binnenhof in The Hague*, 1620-1630, The Hague, Gemeentearchief, reproduced in Richard J. Wattenmaker *et al.*, *Opkomst en bloei van het Noordnederlandse stadsgezicht in de 17de eeuw/ The Dutch Cityscape in the 17th Century and Its Sources* (Amsterdam, Toronto, 1977), cat. no. 50.

[27] *Der Fluyten Lust-hof* is depicted in several Collier paintings; see Edwart Collier, *Vanitas*, 1662, Private Collection, on loan to the Minneapolis Instute of Art, reproduced in *Hoogsteder*, fig. 18. On Collier, see Maarten Wurfbain, 'Collier, Edwart,' in Grove's *Art*, vol. 7, 568-569; *Hoogsteder*, 181. The book entitled *Der Fluyten Lust-hof*, depicted in the 1662 *Vanitas*, is in a slightly different format than the second edition published in the facsimile volume, and the music is provided with text underlay, a practice which is not found in the settings in the facsimile volume. These differences may indicate that Collier used a different edition for his model, or that he painted the book from memory.

rare format was apparently a mid-century specialty of van Eyck's publisher, Paulus Matthyszoon, of Amsterdam, who was quite prominent in his trade. It is difficult to gauge the print runs of the various editions. Matthyszoon chose good, clean type, and, to judge from the facsimile, the whole is neatly and clearly printed.[28] The title pages are really quite explicit: "The Flute's Pleasure Garden, planted with Psalms, Pavans, Allemandes, Courants, Ballets, Airs, etc., and the newest tunes, charmingly and artistically embellished with many variations..." (*Der Fluyten Lust-hof*, II, fol. i *r*, 1654). The work is an anthology of tunes, none of them apparently by van Eyck, and each one is provided with his divisions. The author of the major study on van Eyck's wind music describes the work as a 'pleasant miscellany,' the tunes arranged in no particular order, but according to variety.[29] Each book opens with a free composed prelude (II adds a phantasia), followed with a psalm setting, and the final setting is also of a psalm (See note 29). Dances march in number beside psalm tunes in a mix that might not have brought comfort to some Calvinists, but these were unlikely to venture to the Janskerkhof in the closing light of day.

A large, but by no means predominant portion of the melodies are Calvinist psalms.[30] The largest group of tunes originated as French

The use of *Der Fluyten Lust-hof* in a *vanitas* of the 1660s may indicate that it had recently lost whatever currency, or popularity it had enjoyed, and was thus a suitable symbol of worldly transience.

[28] Van Baak Griffioen, *Jacob van Eyck*, 46, notes that there are many errors in the musical text of *Der Fluyten Lust-hof*. Care must be taken, however, not to equate the accuracy of the internal features of a text with the quality of its external features. The 'Book of Kells' (Dublin, Trinity College, MS 58 (*olim* A. 1. 6), Iona, *ca.* 800) is a spectacular case in point; see Patrick McGurk, 'The Gospel Text,' in *The Book of Kells, MS 58, Trinity College Library Dublin: Commentary*, ed. Peter Fox (Lucerne, 1990), 59-152.

[29] Van Baak Griffioen, *Jacob van Eyck*, 57-58. The items in the de Sany carillon book are arranged much more strictly; the order is partly according to the liturgical year, and partly according to function. The sacred pieces are mostly placed before the secular, and the collection ends with sacred pieces.

[30] There is a much higher proportion of the sacred to the secular in the de Sany carillon book, compared to *Der Fluyten Lust-hof*. This difference may be due to the different *destinarii*, and hence use, of the two collections. A codex of van

airs de cour, and dances, followed by lute-songs, ballads, and dances of English origin. There are nearly as many songs of Dutch origin, and only a smattering of songs of Italian, German, or Spanish provenance. The majority of these pieces would have been known to van Eyck, and his audience, as contrafact songs with new Dutch poetic texts. The earliest melody in the collection is clearly medieval, and the latest can be dated within the half-decade preceeding publication, but most are from the period 1597-1645. How are the tunes treated?

Episodic construction, with violent contrast between sections based on rhythmic patterns and *tempi*, audacious harmonic movement, and programmatic writing, an aural Caravaggesque *chiaroscuro*, almost all these characteristics of the first period of the baroque in music are wanting in van Eyck's settings. No baroque drama, few contrasts, no succession of strong affects. Instead a calm, unified rhythmic motion throughout entire settings, and division figures which are the stock and trade of the sixteenth-century art of diminution. The diminutions on 'Puer nobis nascitur' show this. It is one of the oldest tunes in the collection, and is of German origin; it probably dates from the mid-fourteenth century [music example 1: 'Puer nobis nascitur,' *Der Fluyten Lust-hof*, II, fols. 45*v*-46*r*].[31] For a setting of the mid-seventeenth century, this seems an unremarkably conservative treatment. One is nearly tempted to say that the style, indeed, would have been unremarkable in the days of William the Silent.

Many of the tunes properly belong to the world of the Baroque. The French *airs de cour*, and many of the courants and ballets hail direct from the court of Louis XIII (*e.g.*, 'Courant, of Ach treurt myn bedroefde,' *Der Fluyten Lust-hof*, I, fols. 15*v*-16*r*, whose tune is 'Ah que le ciel est contraire ma vie,' by François Chancy (1635); or 'Aerdigh Martyntje,' *Der Fluyten Lust-hof*, I, fols. 11*r*-12*r*, based on Estienne Moulinié's 'Voyci tantost la froidure bannie' (1629)). That very model of early monody from our textbooks, Giulio Caccini's

Eyck's carillon music, if it should exist, would probably have the same proportion of sacred to secular as the de Sany collection.

[31] On 'Puer nobis nascitur,' see the commentary in *The New Oxford Book of Carols*, ed. Hugh Keyte and Andrew Parrott, with associate editor Clifford Bartlett (Oxford, 1992), no. 21, 67. Van Eyck, of course, did not get his version of the tune from a medieval source, but he may very well have been aware of the tune's relative antiquity.

'Amarilli mia bella,' from his *Le nuove musiche* (Florence, 1601 = 1602 new style), is present in no fewer than three different settings (*Der Fluyten Lust-hof*, I, fols. 42*v*-43*v*, 74*v*-75*v*, and 94*v*-95*r*).[32] The attention the tune receives here is no doubt due to its popularity on a local, domestic level, as was the case throughout most of Western Europe, rather than to its embodying the new ideas of text presentation of Bardi's *Camerata*, or because 'Amarilli' came from the same *milieu* as early opera. Only one of the variations in one of the settings recalls the world from which the tune sprang; and it is a remarkably creditable diminution in the very earliest baroque style [music example 2: 'Amarilli mia bella,' *Der Fluyten Lust-hof*, I, modo 4, fol. 75*v*]. This is, however, not really very far from late-renaissance style; it is notable that there is little room for cadential *trillos*. And the shape of the ornaments which we retrospectively hear as baroque are, of course, imposed by the contour of Caccini's melody. This is, arguably, the only variation in this style in the collection.[33] The variation preceeding is in pure sixteenth-century division style [music example 3: 'Amarilli mia bella,' *Der Fluyten Lust-hof*, I, modo 3, fol. 75*r*]. To van Eyck's credit, he uses his melodic formulae intelligently, and with due variety. His divisions are not applied mechanically.

There is one division technique which strikes us as more baroque than renaissance, and that is van Eyck's sequences of broken chords [music example 4: 'Ghy Ridders in het prachtigh Romen,' *Der Fluyten Lust-hof*, I, modo 4, fol. 31*v*]. This last is from a setting of an *air de cour*.

A feature which is attractive to us, and was probably not jarring to the original users of the collection, is its catholicity. The following

---

[32] Giulio Caccini, *Nouve musiche*, Recent Researches in the Music of the Baroque Era, ed. H. Wiley Hitchcock, vol. IX (Madison, 1970), 18, 85-88; pl. II; on Caccini and his book, see Frauke Schmitz, *Giulio Caccini, 'Nuove musiche' (1602/1614): Texte und Musik*, Musikwissenschaftliche Studien, Bd. 17 (Breisgau and Hochschwarzwald, 1995). For an instance of its citation as an *exemplum*, see Nigel Fortune, 'Solo Song,' in *The Age of Humanism 1540-1630*, New Oxford History of Music, vol. IV, ed. Gerald Abraham (Oxford, 1968), 159.

[33] 'Wat zalmen op den Avond doen,' *Der Fluyten Lust-hof*, I, modo 6, fol. 56*v*, and 'Doen Daphne d'over,' I, modo 5, fols. 69*r*-69*v*, are quite different in their effect.

tune, 'Lus de mi alma,' presumably of Spanish derivation, can serve as illustration [music example 5: 'Lus de mi alma,' *Der Fluyten Lust-hof*, I, fol. 44*r*]. The author of the basic study on van Eyck's wind music has gathered the information which makes this tune so interesting an illustration. The earliest trace of it in Holland is its use in a Dutch play of 1634 (Van Baak Griffioen, *Jacob van Eyck*, 213-215, at 213). Even more intriguing, in that very year Constantijn Huygens wrote a love song for his wife, which was a contrafact of this tune; and Huygens' employer, the stadholder Frederick Henry, was at war with Spain (Van Baak Griffioen, *Jacob van Eyck*, 213). Tunes can cross borders with enviable ease and dispatch.

If one were to characterize the political nature of the collection, one's first impulse might be to deny that there was anything to characterize. There seems to be no exclusion along lines of national religious culture. You will recall that many tunes are English, but even more are from the French court, a very Catholic court indeed; and there is the example of 'Lus de mi alma.' There are, however, no religious tunes which are not Calvinist; some, like 'Puer nobis nascitur,' were, of course, also Catholic in use, as they were in origin. 'Wilhelmus van Nassouwen' (*Der Fluyten Lust-hof*, I, fols. 48*v*-49*v*), and 'Prins Robberts Masco' (*Der Fluyten Lust-hof*, I, fols. 89*r-v*, 95*v*-96*r*) could not be more political, the first a contrafact in praise of William the Silent, and the second a march in support of Prince Rupert; yet this class of tune is very rare in van Eyck's work. There is the overwhelming influence of the Dutch song-books to take into account. The proportion of French tunes may owe something to the cultural prestige of French music, though these tunes are also in the Dutch song-books. A rigorous criterion for tune selection based on politics, or religion, is not discernible; rather the criterion of selection seems to have been local fashion, and the compiler's taste. *Der Fluyten Lust-hof* is not the musical equivalent of a portfolio of anti-Spanish and anti-Catholic steel engravings. Can it, then, be characterized as a political document? Yes; it is a work constructed from a moderate, tolerant, Calvinist position, one in which even dances can be published in company with the psalms. Some may wish to see in the tone of *Der Fluyten Lust-hof* a reflection of the tone of Utrecht society, determined in part by the city's plurality, with its approximate third of Catholics, spread throughout that society.[34]

Der Fluyten Lust-hof is a musical document from a culture whose visual vocabulary was rich in symbolism. Though van Eyck was blind, he would know these symbols from their literary existence. What is the symbolism, in the Dutch Baroque, of the wind instruments van Eyck wrote for?

Symbolically, the recorder and flute are pastoral emblems.[35] Seen in the hands of 'classical' shepherds and shepherdesses, the instruments bring to mind the landscape of Arcadia.[36] It is from this Arcadian world, with its affairs of amorous herders, that the recorder and flute acquired their secondary symbolism as sexual signs.[37] This symbolism could be, and was used in contexts disassociated from Arcadia; yet at times a recorder was just a recorder. Many of the

[34] On the population in Utrecht, see Israel, *Dutch Republic*, 381; and for tolerance in Utrecht, 380. An excellent overview of intellectual positions is Jonathan I. Israel, 'Toleration in Seventeenth-Century Dutch and English Thought,' in Jonathan I. Israel, *Conflicts of Empires: Spain, the Low Countries, and the Stuggle for World Supremacy 1585-1713* (London and Rio Grande, 1997), 241-262 (first published in 1994).

[35] See Paul Joannides, 'Titian's "Daphnis and Chloe": a Search for the Subject of a Familiar Masterpiece,' in *Apollo: the International Magazine of the Arts* vol. CXXXIII, no. 352 (June 1991), 374-382, and the literature cited therein.

[36] See Alison McNeil Kettering, *The Dutch Arcadia: Pastoral Art and Its Audience in the Golden Age* (Totowa, Montclair, and Woodbridge, 1983), 63-99, and Ann Jensen Adams, 'Competing Communities in the "Great Bog of Europe": Identity and Seventeenth-Century Dutch Landscape Painting,' in *Landscape and Power*, ed. W. J. T. Mitchell (Chicago and London, 1994), 35-76. For an example, see Jan de Baen, *Pastoral Scene, ca.* 1660-1670, Private Collection, reproduced in *Hoogsteder*, cat. nr. 2. On de Baen, see Rudolf E. O. Ekkart, 'Baen, Jan de,' in Grove's *Art*, vol. 3, 42; *Hoogsteder*, 137.

[37] A famous example is Rembrandt, *The Flute Player*, 1642, Amsterdam. On this image, see the work of Kettering cited in note 47 *supra*; Gary Schwartz, *Rembrandt: All the Etchings Reproduced in True Size* (Maarssen, 1977), B 188. On Rembrandt, see Gary Schwartz, *Rembrandt: His Life, His Paintings* (Harmondsworth, 1985); B. J. Broos *et al.*, 'Rembrandt (Harmensz.) van Rijn,' in Grove's *Art*, vol. 26, 152-179. The literature on Rembrandt seems boundless, but Schwartz' monograph stands out as a first-rate contextual study.

meanings were probably in simultaneous play. Both flute and recorder are found depicted in low, and high company.[38] And the flute had martial associations, which the recorder did not share. It is notable that a goodly number of the tunes which appear in *Der Fluyten Lust-hof* were set to pastoral poems in the Dutch song-books (Van Baak Griffioen, *Jacob van Eyck*, 77-78). Should we then assume that the symbolism of the recorder in graphic art, and in poetry, applied to the actual instruments? More than certainly. The couples who strolled in the Janskerkhof in the evening had read, or sung the pastoral poetry, they were aware of the allusions, they probably had paintings or prints of shepherds and shepherdesses in their homes, they were the shepherds and shepherdesses themselves, who listened to van Eyck play tunes such as 'Philis schoone Herderin,' 'Philis quam Philander,' and the rest (*Der Fluyten Lust-hof*, I, fols. 36*v*-38*r*, and fols. 45*v*-46*r*, repectively). Van Eyck might as well have been Virgil's Tityrus.[39]

---

[38] For the 'German' flute in low company, see Willem Pietersz. Buytewech, *Tavern Scene*, 1616-1624, Bredius Museum, reproduced in *Hoogsteder*, cat. nr. 8; on this image, see *Willem Buytewech 1591-1624* (Rotterdam?, 1974?), 5-7; and on Buytewech, Maria van Berge-Gerbaud, 'Buytewech, Willem (Pietersz.),' in Grove's *Art*, vol. 5, 323-326; *Hoogsteder*, 161. For the flute in more refined company, see Pieter Franchoys, *Two Musicians, ca.* 1630-1640, The Netherlands Office for Fine Arts, on loan to the Gemeentemuseum, Music Department, The Hague, reproduced in *Hoogsteder*, cat. nr. 16; on Franchoys, see Hans Vlieghe, 'Pieter Franchoys,' in Grove's *Art*, vol. 11, 698-699; *Hoogsteder*, 193. For the recorder in low company, see Pieter Duyfhuysen, *Peasant Interior, ca.* 1630-1640, Private Collection, reproduced in *Hoogsteder*, cat. nr. 14; on Duyfhuysen, see *Hoogsteder*, 185. For the recorder in better company, see Dirck Dircksz. Santvoort, *Portrait of Elisabeth Spiegel as Hearing, ca.* 1630-1639, The Cleveland Museum of Art, reproduced in *Hoogsteder*, fig. 16; on Santvoort, see Rudolf E. O. Ekkart, 'Santvoort, Dirck (Dircksz.),' in Grove's *Art*, vol. 27, 805-806.

[39]
You, O Tityrus, recumbent under the cover of the broad beech,
Studying the sylvan muse with your thin reed pipe...
...You, O Tityrus, tranquil in the shade,
Teach the woods to again echo 'comely Amaryllis.'

[Tityre, tu patulae recubans sub tegmine fagi
silvestrem tenui musam meditaris avena...
.. tu, Tityre, lentus in umbra
formosam resonare doces Amaryllida silvas.]

(*Publii Vergilii Maronis Eclogae*, I, 1-2, 4-5).

Before examining how *Der Fluyten Lust-hof* can help us consider the variety of the Baroque, and broaden our perspective, I will return to Constantijn Huygens.

Huygens was an almost superlative example of the cultural virtuoso of his day.[40] Personal secretary to four successive stadtholders, he was one of the greatest Dutch poets of his time, and also a formidible musician, with French and Italian leanings. Huygens, a patron of both Rembrandt and Saenredam, was the patron-dedicatee of *Der Fluyten Lust-hof*. Perhaps van Eyck presumed upon his blood relationship, but perhaps not. There is circumstantial evidence that Huygens would not have appreciated his 'cousin's' musical anthology.[41] There is no

---

From her first rate source study, 'A Field Guide to the Flowers of the *Fluytn Lust-hof*: Notes on the Familiarity of the Tunes Van Eyck Chose,' in *17th Century Recorder*, 159-175, Ruth van Baak Griffioen draws some important conclusions on how Van Eyck's audience may have heard his music. Thiemo Wind, 'Jacob Van Eyck's *Der Fluytn Lust-hof*: Composition, Improvisation, or ...?,' in *17th Century Recorder*, 177-195, at 194, on the other hand, implies that the Janskerkhof audience was relatively unsophisticated.

40 On Huygens, see H. A. Hofman, *Constantijn Huygens (1596-1687): Een christelijk-humanistisch bourgeois-gentilhomme in dienst van het Oranjehuis* (Utrecht, 1983). This study concentrates more on Huygens' political career, than on his varied artistic achievements. For Huygens' as musician, see Randall H. Tollefsen, 'Huygens, Sir Constanijn,' in Grove's *Music and Musicians*, vol. 8, 831-832; Louis Peter Grijp, 'Dutch Music of the Golden Age,' in *Hoogsteder*, 72-74; and, Eva Legêne, "A Foolish Passion for Sweet Harmony": the Musical Instrument Collection of a Compleat [*sic*] Gentleman, a Monarch, and an Artist, in the Seventeenth Century,' in *Hoogsteder*, 82-86; 81.

Huygens was certainly concerned to have himself represented as both the cultivated man, who has used his *otium* wisely, and as the attentive servant of the state, in Thomas Hendricksz. Keyser, *Constantijn Huygens and His Secretary*, 1627, London, National Gallery, reproduced in Christopher Wright, *The Dutch Painters: 100 Seventeenth Century Masters* (London, 1984^2), 127; on de Keyser, see Ann Jensen Adams, 'Thomas (Hendricksz.) de Keyser,' in Grove's *Art*, vol. 18, 10-11.

41 Huygens' famous tract, *Gebruyck of Ongebruyck van 't Orgel inde Kercken der Vereenighde Nederlanden* (Leiden, 1641), which argued from a standpoint of liturgical propriety alone for the use of the organ in congregational Psalm singing, also contains hints as to his opinion of his 'cousin's' work. The following analysis of part of the tract is from Louis Peter Grijp, 'Dutch Music of the Golden Age,' in *Hoogsteder*, 73:

known connection to van Eyck in the following anecdote, but it deserves retelling. On one occasion, after Huygens had performed something, he deflected his auditor's compliment with a variation on the humility *topos*, saying: 'in the land of the blind, the one-eyed man is king.'[42] Huygens, culturally ambitious, could look beyond the borders of Holland for his music. We must, however, consider *Der Fluyten Lust-hof* alongside the other achievements of the Dutch Baroque, the ter Brugghens, Leysters, and Rembrandts.

What is there to learn from *Der Fluyten Lust-hof*? The work was popular, going through at least five editions in just over a decade. A copy of the second edition was in the library of king João IV of Portugal in 1649, and the collection was advertised at the Frankfurt and Leipzig bookfairs three years previously (Van Baak Griffioen, *Jacob van Eyck*, 63). The compiler of the work was a popular performer,

---

However, he [Constantijn Huygens] would prefer to have public recitals dispensed with... Even the variations on psalm melodies, played while people are leaving the church, cannot convert Huygens. He complains of the couplets that the organist 'squeezes into every shape and size imaginable, bending and breaking them on every side' ('In alle vaten van de kunst gegoten, in allerhande swieren gebogen ende gebroken'). The fantasia that the organist performs is derisively referred to by Huygens as the player's 'daydreams.'

Huygens has, with these words, described a considerable portion of the contents of *Der Fluyten Lust-hof*, and its entire style. Van Baak Griffioen's statement, that "...it seems unlikely that *Der Fluyten Lust-hof* would have given him [Huygens] much aesthetic pleasure," seems an understatement (van Baak Griffioen, *Jacob van Eyck*, 61). The evidence she advances for this, based on Huygens' compositional strictures, is rather more paraphrastic than the direct, and blunt statements contained in Huygens' 1641 treatise.

[42] Quoted in Louis Peter Grijp, 'Dutch Music of the Golden Age,' in *Hoogsteder*, 63. Huygens, 'the complete gentleman,' could, on occasion, be narrowly self-serving, petty, and juvenile. The incidents arising from Rembrandt's commission to paint the famous pair of portraits, one of Huygens' brother, Maurits, and the other of the artist Jacques de Gheyn III, clearly demonstrate this. Even if some of the circumstances surrounding the patronage, execution, and reception of Rembrandt's de Gheyn portrait are not clear, Huygens' spiteful Latin verses belittling the work are surprising (Gary Schwartz, *Rembrandt: His Life, His Paintings* (Harmondsworth, 1985), 95-97). Huygens' behaviour in the case of Rembrandt shows what he was capable of; he could, therefore, have had his cousin van Eyck in mind when he quipped about the 'land of the blind.'

eulogized in verse, who played for a fashionable urban audience. Neither he, nor his publications were marginal. He was firmly rooted in his time and place, the Dutch 'Golden Age.' Many of the tunes in his collection had a half-century of use behind them. His presentation of most of the items, even of the baroque ones, strikes us as belonging to the previous cultural period. What are we to do with this seeming contradiction? Treat it as something other than a contradiction. The continuity, indeed the vitality of cultural and artistic processes apparently older than those we imagine are characteristic of particular periods, styles, or movements must be incorporated into our account of those periods, styles, or movements. The instance of van Eyck is not unique. A style of *organum* considered normative for the twelfth-century, and usually termed archaic if found later, was practised in some of the German-language areas of the Empire well into the fifteenth century.[43] It is, after all, somewhat limiting to write the history of culture in the West as a triumphalist history of innovations.

[43] *E.g.*, 'Ad laudes Marie cantemus,' London, British Library, MS add. 27630, 'St. Blasien Troper,' St. Blasien, saec. XV, fol. 45*r*, or 'Alleluia. Dies sanctificatus,' *ibid.*, fol. 47*v*.

musical ex. 1

musical ex. 2

musical ex. 3

musical ex. 4

musical ex. 5

AGMV MARQUIS
Québec, Canada
1999